MW01716841

Free at Last: Ezra & Nehemiah

Jim Dyet

EMMAUS
WORLDWIDE

Developed as a study course by Emmaus Correspondence School, founded in 1942.

Mission

Glorify God by providing biblically sound resources and structured study materials that teach people from every nation to accept Christ as their Savior and Lord, grow in Christ and share their faith with others.

Free at Last: Ezra & Nehemiah

Jim Dyet

Published by:
Emmaus Worldwide
(A division of ECS Ministries)
PO Box 1028
Dubuque, IA 52004-1028
phone: (563) 585-2070
email: info@emmausworldwide.org
website: EmmausWorldwide.org

First Printed 2025 (AK '25)
ISBN 978-1-59387-504-6

Code: FAL

Course Description

The Babylonians had destroyed Jerusalem and its temple and had dragged thousands of Jews into captivity in Babylon. However, the books of Ezra and Nehemiah report the end of the Babylonian Captivity and the Jews' returns to Jerusalem and Judea. The first return occurred around 537 B.C. under Zerubbabel, who led the rebuilding of the temple. The second return took place under Ezra in 458 B.C. whose task was to beautify the temple and lead a revival. Nehemiah led the third return in 444 B.C. to rebuild Jerusalem's walls that the Babylonians had destroyed.

The books of Ezra and Nehemiah reveal God's faithfulness to keep His promises. In turn, His people should place their confidence in Him, be thankful for His care, obey Him, and serve Him faithfully.

Lessons You Will Study

1. Free to Return Home 7
2. Progress, Opposition, and Divine Intervention 13
3. The Temple Is Completed and the Passover Is Observed 21
4. Ezra Returns from Captivity 29
5. Sin and Confession 37
6. The Power of Prayer 45
7. No Situation Is Too Hard for God to Handle 51
8. Organized to Rebuild Jerusalem's Walls 59
9. Dealing with Ridicule, Hostility, and Domestic Crises 67
10. Conspiracy, but the Work Gets Finished 75
11. The Power of God's Word 83
12. Settling Down and Taking Responsibility 91

Student Instructions

This Emmaus course is designed to help you know God through a better understanding of the Bible and know it applies to your life. However, this course can never take the place of the Bible itself. The Bible is inexhaustible, and no course can give the full meaning of its truth. If simply studying this course is the end goal, it will become an obstacle to your growth; if it is used to inspire and equip you for your own personal study of the Bible, then it will achieve its goal. As you study the Bible using this course, prayerfully ask God to reveal His truth to you in a powerful way.

Course Sections

This course has three parts: the *lessons*, the *exams* and the *answer sheet*.

The Lessons

Each lesson is written to help explain truths from the Bible. Read each lesson through at least twice—once to get a general idea of its content, then again, slowly, looking up any Bible references given. You should always have your Bible opened to the verses or passage being studied. It is important that you read the Bible passages referenced, as some questions in the exams may be based on the Bible text.

To look up a Bible verse, keep in mind that passages in the Bible are listed by book, chapter, and verse. For instance, 2 Peter 1:21 refers to the second book of Peter, chapter 1, and verse 21. At the beginning of every Bible, there is a table of contents which lists the names of the books of the Bible and tells the page number on which each book begins. For practice, look up 2 Peter in the table of contents, turn to the page number listed, then find the chapter and verse.

The Exams

At the end of each lesson, there is an exam to assess your knowledge of the course material and the Bible passages. The exams contain multiple choice and/or True/False (T/F) questions. After you have studied a lesson, complete the exam for that lesson by recording your answers on the exam sheet that has been provided. If you have difficulty answering the questions, re-read the lesson or use the Bible as a reference.

Please note, it is best not to answer the questions based on what you *think* or have *always believed*. The questions are designed to find out if you understand the material in the course and the Bible.

What Do You Say?

In addition to the multiple choice section, each exam also contains a *What Do You Say?* question. These questions are designed for your personal reflection and to help you express your ideas and feelings as you process the lesson's content.

The Answer Sheet

Use the answer sheet provided by your group leader or instructor. When you have determined the right answer to a question on an exam, fill in the corresponding letter on the answer sheet. If you do not have someone who could provide an answer sheet, you can download one at www.emmausworldwide.org/answersheets

Submitting the Answer Sheet

When you have answered all the exam questions on the answer sheet, check them carefully. Fill in your contact information and submit your completed answer sheet to your group leader or instructor or the organization from which you received it.

OPTION 1: Send to your group leader or instructor

If you know your group leader or instructor, give them your completed answer sheet or mail it to the address listed here (if blank, go to option 2).

OPTION 2: Send to Emmaus Worldwide's head office

If no address is listed above, or if you do not know if you have a group leader or instructor and are unsure of where to send your answer sheet, choose one of the following:

MAIL the exam sheet to

Emmaus Worldwide
PO Box 1028
Dubuque, IA 52004-1028

EMAIL the exam sheet to

Exams@EmmausWorldwide.org

Receiving Your Results

You will receive back your graded exam sheet (through the same method it was submitted, either mail or email), including your final grade and a personal response from your group leader or instructor or a representative of Emmaus Worldwide.

LESSON 1

Free to Return Home

Ezra 1—2

Introduction

There is something special about being home. Home is a place that represents where we belong, where we rest, and where we are most connected in our closest relationships. Home is a place of freedom. From early in Genesis, the Bible tells us the story of God calling Abram out of his home and on to another home that God promised to give to him and his children. We then read how God supplied those people, later known as the Jews, with this promised homeland, and how they became His people. Unfortunately, this freedom was not to last.

Because God's people, the Jews, broke His laws, refused to observe the Sabbath, and bowed down to idols, God sent powerful, cruel nations against them. The Northern Kingdom of Israel felt the first stroke of God's punishment in 721 B.C., when the Assyrians swept down upon it and carried the ten tribes of Israel into captivity. The Southern Kingdom, Judah, felt the second stroke of God's punishment, when the Babylonians leveled Jerusalem and the temple and deported numerous Jews, including the leaders, to Babylon. The deportations occurred in 605, 597, and 586 B.C. However, God had said that the Captivity would last 70 years and then the captives would return home (Jeremiah 25:11; 29:10). He even predicted the name of Cyrus, the ruler who would allow the captives to return home (Isaiah 44:28; 45:1, 13).

The first chapter of Ezra reveals the fulfilment of God's promise to return His people to their homeland when Cyrus ruled the land of captivity. The second chapter lists those who returned home.

Cyrus's proclamation (1:1,2)

Cyrus was the Persian king who defeated the Babylonians and ended their empire in 539 B.C. The account of this historic defeat of Babylon is fascinating.

Cyrus had laid siege to Babylon, but the city had stored enough supplies to last twenty years. Furthermore, the Euphrates River ran through the city, so there was plenty of water for the people. However, the Persian army devised a way to conquer Babylon. They dug a canal that diverted the water into a lake north of Babylon. The soldiers were then able to march into the city by night on the dry riverbed and under the sluice gate. This enabled the Persians to launch a surprise attack and overthrow the Babylonians in 539 B.C. The downfall of Babylon was prophesied. In Isaiah 47:11, God said concerning Babylon: "Disaster shall fall upon you, for which you will not be able to atone; and ruin shall come upon you suddenly, of which you know nothing."

Because he was a polytheist (someone who believed in the existence of territorial gods), Cyrus wanted to gain the favor of the Jews' God. Therefore, in his first year, he decreed that the Jews be allowed to return to Jerusalem to build a house for their God. Of course, God had planned to use Cyrus for this purpose. He had promised all this in Isaiah 44:28; 45:1, 13 and Jeremiah 25:11; 29:10.

Just as God's Word came true in the case of Cyrus, we can continue to trust all that God says in the Bible. In his letter to a young pastor named Titus, the apostle Paul writes that God cannot lie (Titus 1:2). Human beings often lie, but God is truthful and therefore may be trusted. Psalm 118:8 advises: "It is better to take refuge in the Lord than to trust in man." Deuteronomy 7:7-16 tells us that God delivered the Jews from Egypt to show His faithfulness. He did not choose them because they were better than others in some way, but because He loved them. Even though they were unfaithful, He was faithful, and we can trust Him to keep His promises.

Assistance for the returnees (1:3–11)

Not only did Cyrus decree the return of the Jews to Jerusalem but he also ordered people along the way to Jerusalem to supply the returnees with goods, animals, and offerings for the house of God in Jerusalem.

The Jews' leaders, the priests and the Levites, and all whom God had inspired to return to Jerusalem received help from their Persian neighbors and even from Cyrus. Cyrus returned objects that the Babylonians had taken from the temple when they destroyed it. Ezra numbered these objects as 2,499 and the number of gold and silver items at 5,400. Cyrus put Mithredath in charge of these treasures, and in turn Mithredath counted them out to Sheshbazzar, the prince of Judah.

Something similar to the Persians' giving gifts to the Jewish exiles occurred centuries earlier. God's people, the Israelites, had been slaves in Egypt for a long time, and their task masters beat them and overworked them, but they cried out to the Lord, and He answered them. At the hand of Moses, the Lord delivered His people and set them free. Before the Israelites left Egypt, the Egyptians feared them and gave them riches and clothing. Exodus 12:35, 36 reports: "The people of Israel . . . had asked the Egyptians for silver and gold jewelry and for clothing. And the Lord had given the people favor in the sight of the Egyptians, so that they let them have what they asked. Thus they plundered the Egyptians."

If we are trusting the Lord, we can claim His promise to meet all our needs. Matthew 6:33 tells us to "seek first the kingdom of God and his righteousness, and all these things will be added to you." The apostle James wrote: "Every good gift and every perfect gift is from above, coming down from the Father of lights, with whom there is no variation or shadow due to change" (James 1:17). Even if we live from hand to mouth, we can be grateful that it is God's hand and our mouth.

List of returning exiles (2:1–70)

Ezra is believed to have written the book of Ezra. He was not only a priest but also a scribe (Ezra 7:11). A priest was responsible to lead God's people in worship. A scribe was responsible to teach God's Law. A scribe also meticulously wrote portions of Scripture. We can appreciate Ezra's work of listing in detail "the people of the province [Judah] who came up out of captivity of those exiles whom Nebuchadnezzar the king of Babylon had carried captive to Babylonia" (2:1).

First on the list are prominent leaders. Zerubbabel led the expedition. Jeshua, also known as Joshua, was the high priest. Nehemiah was a different person from the Nehemiah who led the building of Jerusalem's walls. Mordecai was not the Mordecai mentioned in the book of Esther. The rest of the men named in verse two were likely prominent leaders.

In 2:1–35 Ezra listed people in general. Next, he listed the priests (2:36–39), and the Levites (2:40–54). They were a tribe set aside for service in the tabernacle and later the temple. Then he lists the descendants of King Solomon's servants (2:55–58). Those who could not clearly trace their ancestry completed the list (2:59–63). Altogether, the number of returnees totaled 29,829. The number 42,360 in verse 64 may include the wives and children of the returning exiles. Even the exiles' servants, singers, horses, mules, camels, and donkeys were numbered (2:65–67).

When the exiles returned home, they gave generously to the project of rebuilding the temple, and they settled in their ancestral towns and villages (2:68–70).

While reading these lists of names may feel strange to us, they are a beautiful picture of how God remembers each individual person, and the attention He pays to each of our lives. Several other lists of God's people may be found in the Bible, but let us just mention two. Hebrews 11, often called the Hall of Faith chapter of the Bible, lists believers whose faith triumphed over severe circumstances, even martyrdom. The second list is found in the Book of Life. This is a list of those who believed on Jesus as their Savior. At the last judgment, the Great White Throne Judgment, those whose names are not in the book of life are cast into the lake of fire (Revelation 20:15). It is of the utmost importance to believe on Jesus and spend eternity in heaven instead of in the lake of fire.

Is your name written in the Book of Life?

LESSON 1 EXAM

Use the answer sheet that has been provided to complete your exam.

1. What is the primary reason God allowed the Jews to be taken into captivity?

A. They ignored the Sabbath and worshipped idols
B. They rejected the leadership of their kings
C. They had disobeyed the prophet Jeremiah
D. They were too weak to defend themselves

2. Which ruler allowed the Jews to return to their homeland and rebuild the temple?

A. Nebuchadnezzar
B. Darius
C. Cyrus
D. Xerxes

3. What historical event enabled the Persian army to conquer Babylon?

A. A long siege that eventually led to starvation
B. A surprise attack during a festival
C. Diverting the Euphrates River and entering through the dry riverbed
D. The Babylonians opening the gates in fear of defeat

4. What was the reason Cyrus wanted to support the return of the Jews to Jerusalem?

A. He feared the Jews would revolt
B. He wanted to gain the favor of the Jewish God
C. He sought to expand his empire by strengthening alliances
D. He believed it was a way to enrich Persia

5. The Jews were in captivity

A. 40 years
B. 7 years
C. 12 Months
D. 70 years

6. What did the Persian king Cyrus return to the Jews that had been taken by the Babylonians?

A. The gold and silver of the Babylonian temples
B. Objects from the temple in Jerusalem

C. The sacred writings of the Jews
D. Land grants for farming

7. What important event in Israel's history is similar to the Persian support for the Jews' return?

A. The Israelites' escape from Egypt
B. The conquest of Canaan
C. The establishment of the Davidic kingdom
D. The rebuilding of the walls of Jerusalem under Nehemiah

8. How many people are listed as returning exiles in the book of Ezra?

A. 42,360
B. 29,829
C. 6,000
D. 1,000

9. What was Ezra's role in relation to the Jews' return to Jerusalem?

A. He was a political leader who governed the people
B. He was a wealthy merchant who funded the return
C. He was a military leader who fought to defend Jerusalem
D. He was a priest and scribe who taught God's law

10. What does the list of returning exiles in Ezra symbolize for us today?

A. The wealth of God's people
B. The political power of Israel
C. The detailed record of God's faithfulness to each individual
D. The victory of the Jews over their enemies

What Do You Say?

How do you see God's faithfulness in the return of the exiles to Jerusalem, and what does this teach us about trusting God with the promises He has made in our own lives?

___

___

___

LESSON 2

Progress, Opposition, and Divine Intervention

Ezra 3:1—6:12

Introduction

Those who journeyed home from captivity demonstrated a strong faith in the Lord. They could have remained in Babylon, built homes, and planted gardens. But obeying the Lord was more important to them than physical comfort. Also, their hearts were in Jerusalem, not in Babylon. So, they braved the hazardous, tiring 900 mile journey to Jerusalem.

This section illustrates that obeying the Lord may not always be easy, but it is always the right thing to do.

Worship according to the Law of Moses (3:1–7)

The Jews who returned home settled in towns around Jerusalem. However, in the seventh month, which was September–October, they assembled in Jerusalem in full agreement to rebuild the temple (3:1). The first project was that of building the altar. Jeshua, the high priest, his fellow priests, Zerubbabel and his relatives took on the project, and determined to offer burnt offerings on it in compliance with the instructions found in the Law of Moses (3:2).

Following the Law of Moses was extremely important to the former captives. Their forefathers had broken the Law of Moses and therefore had brought the Captivity on themselves. The returnees did not want to follow their forefathers' bad example and face a similar punishment. Obeying God's Word ranks far above simply knowing it. Jesus told His followers, "You are my friends if you do what I command you" (John 15:14).

The returnees feared their pagan neighbors whom the Assyrians had placed in Judah years ago, but they feared God more than their pagan neighbors. Therefore, they continued the building project by setting the altar in its place and offering burnt offerings on it to the Lord (Ezra 3:3).

The regulations concerning burnt offerings are found in Leviticus 1:3–17. The offering could be a bull, a sheep, a goat, or birds. The priests were instructed to kill the animal or bird and burn all of it on the altar as an offering to the Lord. The Jews referred to in Ezra 3:2, 3 presented their burnt offerings to the Lord in the morning and in the evening. These many sacrifices might seem strange to us, but they show us the cost of sin. Christians now can look to Jesus as the sacrifice that fulfilled the payment that all of these sacrifices pointed to. Hebrews 10:12-14 tells us that "But this Man, after He had offered one sacrifice for sins forever, sat down at the right hand of God...by one offering He has perfected forever those who are being sanctified."

The returnees also kept the Feast of Booths on days 15–21 of the seventh month (Leviticus 23:33–36, 39–43; Numbers 29:12–39). This feast was the third of three annual festivals that the male Jews celebrated. For seven days they lived in booths made from the branches of trees. The returnees were careful to do this as the Law of Moses required, offering sacrifices by number. Unger's Bible Dictionary (p.360) lists the seven days of required sacrifices as follows:

Day one: 13 bulls, 2 rams, 14 lambs, 1 goat
Day two: 12 bulls, 2 rams, 14 lambs, 1 goat
Day three: 11 bulls, 2 rams, 14 lambs, 1 goat
Day four: 10 bulls, 2 rams, 14 lambs, 1 goat
Day five: 9 bulls, 2 rams, 14 lambs, 1 goat
Day six: 8 bulls, 2 rams, 14 lambs, 1 goat
Day seven: 7 bulls, 2 rams, 14 lambs, 1 goat
Total 70 bulls 14 rams 98 lambs 7 goats

From the first day of the seventh month the priests continued to offer burnt offerings and other offerings as well as the freewill offerings of the people (3:5, 6). But they still had not laid the foundation of the temple (3:6). Therefore, they hired Sidonians and Tyrians to bring cedars from Lebanon to Joppa, the seaport (3:7).

The foundation is laid (3:8–13)

Seventy years after the Babylonians deported Jews from Jerusalem, Zerubbabel and Jeshua organized the Levites and others to supervise the building of the temple (3:8–9). When the builders completed the foundation, a joyful celebration followed. The priests, Levites, and appointed singers praised the Lord and thanked Him with trumpets, cymbals, and responsive singing. They proclaimed the Lord's goodness and endless love, and all the people shouted loud praises to the Lord, because the foundation was laid (3:10–11).

A firm foundation is vitally important to a building. It gives the building stability and security. The apostle Paul identified Jesus Christ as the only foundation on which the church is built (1 Corinthians 3:11). If you have built your life on Jesus Christ as your Savior, you can weather the storms that target you. Jesus will keep you safe and stable. See Matthew 7:24, 25.

In spite of the joyful celebration, many of the elderly men wept loudly. They had seen the former temple that the Babylonians destroyed 50 years earlier. Likely, they realized that the new temple was not going to be as big as the former one. People far away heard the loud weeping mingled with the loud shouts of praise (Ezra 3:13).

Angry neighbors stop construction (4:1–24)

The returnees had enemies. They were Gentile neighbors who wanted to disrupt the building of the temple. First, they asked Zerubbabel to let them join in the building of the temple. They claimed to worship God, saying they had been worshiping Him and sacrificing to Him since the King of Assyria had transplanted them in Judah (4:1, 2). This settling of the Gentiles in Judah happened in 722 B.C. (see 2 Kings 17:23, 24). To his credit, Zerubbabel, Jeshua, and the rest of the returnees' leaders rejected the Gentile neighbors' request (Ezra 4:3). They must have believed the Gentiles hoped to join the work crew in order to sabotage the building project. Besides, King Cyrus had specifically charged the Jews with the responsibility to rebuild the temple (1:3).

Next, the enemies discouraged and intimidated the people of Judah. They kept on doing this until Darius was King of Persia, and even bribed men to falsely accuse the builders (4:5). Then, when Ahasuerus was King of Persia, they sent a letter of accusation against the returnees (4:6).

Furthermore, the enemies, Rehum and Shimshai, sent a letter to Artaxerxes of Persia in which they accused the Jews of rebelling. They told the king that the Jews would refuse to pay tribute, custom, or toll when the city and its walls were rebuilt. They invited the king to search the historical records and see that Jerusalem was a rebellious and seditious city. They added that once the city and walls are rebuilt, the king will lose the land beyond the Euphrates River (4:7–16).

King Artaxerxes replied to the Jews' enemies. He agreed with their accusations and warnings about the Jews (4:17–20) and issued a decree that the rebuilding effort stop (4:21). He ordered the accusers to waste no time in enforcing the decree (4:22). Two of the enemies, Rehum and Shimshai, and their companions rushed to Jerusalem and forced the Jews to stop rebuilding (4:23). It did not resume until the second year of King Darius's reign (4:24).

The rebuilding gets a fresh start (5:1—17)

Evil men cannot win over God. God dispatched two prophets, Haggai and Zechariah, to preach to the Jews and encourage them to resume the rebuilding project (5:1). Zerubbabel and Jeshua accepted the challenge and began to rebuild the temple (5:2). Read Haggai 1:14; Zechariah 4:8, 9; 6:15 to see what Haggai and Zechariah wrote about the temple.

Once again, the workers faced opposition to the rebuilding of the temple. Tattenai, the governor of a large area that included Judah, his assistant Shethar-Bozeni, and their associates demanded to know where the temple workers got the permission to build the temple (5:3). They also asked for the names of the workers (5:4). Courageously the builders continued under God's watchful eye, while they waited for word from King Darius (5:5).

According to Ezra 5:6–17, Tattenai and his colleagues sent a letter to King Darius. They told him the temple workers were working diligently and making progress. They reported that the workers had identified themselves as servants of the God of heaven and earth. The workers had also reviewed the temple's history from the time of King Solomon, "a great king of Israel" (5:11), to its destruction by Nebuchadnezzar, to King Cyrus's decree to rebuild it and to the laying of its foundation.

The letter closed with an appeal to Darius to search the archives to see whether Cyrus had issued a decree to rebuild the temple.

Darius sides with the returnees (6:1–12)

Darius searched the archives and found Cyrus's decree to rebuild the temple and return the temple's vessels that Nebuchadnezzar had stolen (6:1–5). Darius told Tattenai and his men to take a hands-off approach to the rebuilding effort (6:6, 7). He also decreed that Tattenai pay the builders of the temple in full out of the royal treasury and give the priests whatever they needed for offerings and sacrifices (6:8–10). Darius's letter issued a warning. Whoever disobeyed the decree would be impaled on a beam from his house and his house would be demolished (6:11). He closed by acknowledging that God had chosen to dwell in the temple (6:12).

When you serve the Lord, keep in mind that those who oppose you may be powerful, but God is all-powerful. 1 Corinthians 15:58 tells us to be "steadfast, immovable, always abounding in the work of the Lord, knowing that in the Lord your labor is not in vain."

LESSON 2 EXAM

Use the answer sheet that has been provided to complete your exam.

1. Why did the Jews who returned from captivity choose to travel 900 miles to Jerusalem?

A. To build their homes and gardens
B. To establish a new kingdom
C. To obey God's command to rebuild the temple
D. To escape the harsh rule of the Babylonians

2. What was the first task that the returnees undertook upon arriving in Jerusalem?

A. Rebuilding their homes
B. Offering sacrifices
C. Rebuilding the temple foundation
D. Building the altar

3. Why was it important for the returnees to follow the Law of Moses when rebuilding the altar?

A. To avoid repeating the mistakes of their ancestors
B. To gain favor with the Persian king
C. To impress their neighbors
D. To attract new followers to Judaism

4. How did the returnees respond to the fear of their pagan neighbors?

A. They abandoned the building project
B. They asked the neighbors for help in building
C. They compromised with their neighbors to avoid conflict
D. They ignored their neighbors and continued to work

5. What was the significance of the burnt offerings offered on the altar?

A. They were a celebration of their return home
B. They were an attempt to appease the Persian king
C. They were a way to make peace with their neighbors
D. They symbolized the cost of sin and obedience to God

6. Which Jewish festival did the returnees observe after rebuilding the altar?

A. Passover
B. Feast of Booths
C. Day of Atonement
D. Feast of Weeks

7. Why did the enemies of the returnees want to stop the rebuilding of the temple?

A. They were jealous of the Jews' progress
B. They feared the Jews would become too powerful
C. They wanted to take control of the project for themselves
D. They disagreed with the religious practices of the Jews

8. How did King Artaxerxes respond to the accusations made against the Jews by their enemies?

A. He ordered the rebuilding of the temple to continue immediately
B. He sided with the Jews and ordered their enemies to cease opposition
C. He issued a decree for the rebuilding to stop
D. He allowed the Jews to continue but with restrictions

9. Who did God send to encourage the returnees to continue rebuilding the temple?

A. Moses and Elijah
B. Haggai and Zechariah
C. Jeremiah and Daniel
D. Zerubbabel and Jeshua

10. God affirmed his hand on the project by

A. Judging Tattenai
B. Providing rich Jews to fund the project
C. Sending soldiers to rescue the Jews
D. Giving it the full support of a Gentile king and his resources.

What Do You Say?

How do you see God's timing and provision in your own life during times of waiting or uncertainty?

LESSON 3

The Temple Is Completed and the Passover Is Observed

Ezra 6:13-22

Introduction

Completing a project brings great satisfaction to those who started it. Perhaps you started a job and received an assignment. Weren't you happy that you completed the assignment in good order? Or you may have completed a course in school that required a lot of memorization and studying. When you successfully finished the course, you were happy. This lesson focuses on the completed foundation of the temple in Jerusalem and the joy that many of the returnees experienced.

Compliance (6:13–15)

The Lord intervened on behalf of His people by causing Darius, King of Persia, to order the rebuilding of the temple to resume. He even decreed that the builders get paid from the royal treasury and receive everything they needed to present offerings to the God of heaven. This decree turned Governor Tattenai and his men from hindrances to the building of the temple to helpers. They diligently obeyed Darius's decree (6:13).

The elders of the Jews built and prospered during Haggai and Zechariah's preaching. They completed the work of building the temple that God and the Persians kings had ordered (6:14, 15). God always finishes what He begins. He can even move the hearts and minds of kings to comply with His will.

Celebration (6:16–22)

Now, it was time to celebrate. The people of Israel, the priests, the Levites, and the rest of the returnees joyfully celebrated the dedication of the temple (6:16). Finally, after decades of captivity with no central place to gather to worship the Lord, now they can meet together and anticipate worshiping together in a new temple. Christians should joyfully celebrate what God has done in our lives and the fellowship we enjoy as we worship together. Every day we can celebrate the things we have because of Jesus' completed work. He has forgiven our sins, given us eternal life, and made us members of His family (Ephesians 1:7; John 3:16; 10:28; 1 John 3:1).

The Jews' celebration included numerous offerings. Ezra 6:17 lists 100 bulls, 200 rams, 400 lambs, 12 male goats as a sin offering, and one goat for each of the tribes of Israel. This mention of 12 male goats, "according to the number of the tribes of Israel" shows us that the tribes were not lost, as some people believe. The twelve tribes will certainly continue, and are even seen clearly in the last days when all the tribes are sealed during the tribulation (Revelation 7:1–8).

During the dedication of the temple, the people of Israel commissioned the priests and the Levites to serve God, according to what was specified in the Law of Moses (Ezra 6:18). After 70 years of captivity for failing to keep the Law, they were eager to get things right! They had endured the punishment for their sins, and now were motivated to follow God's Word for their good. While we rely on the grace of God as believers, we know that God will discipline His children (Hebrews 12:5-7).

The Jews had not celebrated the Passover since they were taken into captivity. Now, they were back in Jerusalem, and they had rebuilt the temple. It was the fourteenth day of the new year—time to celebrate the Passover (Ezra 6:19)! Having purified themselves, the priests and the Levites sacrificed the Passover lamb for all the returnees, for their fellow priests, and for themselves (6:20).

The Passover marked the beginning of a new year (Exodus 12:2). Similarly, when a person believes on Jesus as his Savior, Jesus frees him from slavery to sin with the payment of His blood. The salvation experience is the beginning of a brand-new life. 2 Corinthians 5:17 declares, "Therefore, if anyone is in Christ, he is a new creation. The old has passed away; behold, the new has come."

The Passover explained

The Passover commemorated the Jews' exodus from Egypt. The account of the first Passover is found in Exodus 10-12. The Jews were slaves in Egypt. Their taskmasters treated them cruelly. They beat them and forced them into hard labor. But the Jewish slaves cried out to the Lord, and He responded by appointing Moses and Aaron to be His representatives to tell Pharaoh, the Egyptian ruler, "Let my people go." When Pharaoh refused, the Lord sent ten plagues to punish and persuade Pharaoh to set the people free. The Passover preceded the tenth plague.

The Lord instructed His people to take one lamb per household (Exodus 12:3). The lamb was to be a year-old male without blemish (12:5). At twilight on the fourteenth day of the month, every family was required to kill its lamb and smear some of its blood on the doorposts and lintel (12:6, 7). The families were instructed to roast the whole lamb and eat it with unleavened bread and bitter herbs (12:8, 9). They were also instructed to burn leftovers the next morning (12:10). Furthermore, they were required to eat the lamb quickly and be ready to depart (12:11).

The Lord explained that He would pass over Egypt that night and strike all the firstborn in Egypt, but He would pass over every house that displayed the blood of the lamb and not strike it (12:12, 13). He said Israel was to keep the Passover feast annually throughout all generations (12:14). As a follow-up to the Passover, the Lord told the Israelites to eat unleavened (without yeast) bread for seven days (12:15).

When the Lord smote all the firstborn in Egypt where the lamb's blood was not applied, Pharaoh let the Jews leave Egypt (12:12; 29–32).

The New Testament identifies Jesus as our Passover Lamb, who was sacrificed for us (1 Corinthians 5:7). John the Baptist pointed to Jesus and said, "Behold the Lamb of God, who takes away the sin of the world" (John 1:29). Just as the Jews were slaves in Egypt, so is everyone a slave to sin until Jesus sets him free (see Romans 6:17, 18). Every Jewish family was delivered from Egypt at the cost of a spotless lamb's blood, and apostle Peter wrote that believers were "ransomed [purchased] . . . not with perishable things such as silver and gold, but with the precious blood of Christ, like that of a lamb without blemish or spot" (1 Peter 1:18, 19). Revelation 1:5 tells us that Jesus "loved us and washed us from our sins in His own blood."

Jesus pictured the Passover lamb perfectly. He even fulfilled the requirement the Lord gave the Jews to not break any of the lamb's bones (Exodus 12:46). When Jesus was on the cross along with two criminals, soldiers broke the criminals' legs to hasten their death so they would not remain on the crosses on the Sabbath. However, when they came to Jesus, they saw that He was dead already, so they did not break His legs (John 19:31–33). John reports, "For these things took place that the Scripture might be fulfilled: 'Not one of his bones will be broken'" (19:36).

No one is excluded from the Bible's invitation to believe on Jesus and be made free from sin and eternal punishment. John 3:16 proclaims, "For God so loved the world, hat he gave his only Son, that whoever believes in him should not perish but have eternal life." Jesus promised: "If the Son sets you free, you will be free indeed" (8:36). Jesus even saved the apostle Paul, who called himself "the foremost of sinners" (see 1 Timothy 1:13–15).

The Passover feast (6:21-22)

Ezra 6:21 identifies those who ate the Passover feast after the temple was dedicated. The participants were the returnees from the captivity and Jews who had not been taken into captivity and had repented of their unholy involvement with the pagan practices of their Gentile neighbors. These people had, therefore, separated themselves from the uncleanness of their Gentile neighbors in order to worship the God of Israel. Those who had done wrong and repented were able to experience the joy of this feast. As we repent and are forgiven, God restores joy. He will not cast off forever. We see even for the returnees that the nation was regaining its joy in God, though they had sinned before. In all of God's punishment, it was His ultimate purpose for them to return to Him and cherish Him as they ought.

In accordance with the Law of Moses, the worshipers kept the Feast of Unleavened Bread seven days. Subsequently, God made the worshipers joyful. We should not be surprised that God made His people joyful. Joy follows obedience. Jesus promised that keeping His commandments brings joy to those who keep them (John 15:10, 11).

God is identified in 6:22 as the God who had persuaded the King of Assyria, Darius, to decree the resumption of the temple's building project. Proverbs 21:1 says, "The king's heart is a stream of water in the hand of the LORD; he turns it wherever he will." At times, a nation's head of state may make it difficult for Christians to worship and do what is right, but the Lord can intervene. He can change the heart of a nation's head of state and bring about favorable conditions. The apostle Paul instructs believers to pray for kings and all who are in high positions (1 Timothy 2:1, 2).

LESSON 3 EXAM

Use the answer sheet that has been provided to complete your exam.

1. Who intervened on behalf of the Israelites to ensure the completion of the temple?

A. Darius, King of Persia
B. Haggai
C. Zerubbabel
D. Tattenai

2. What role did the prophets Haggai and Zechariah play in the rebuilding of the temple?

A. They opposed the rebuilding project
B. They encouraged the people to continue the work
C. They preached and encouraged the builders
D. They were responsible for designing the temple

3. Who said, "Behold, the Lamb of God, who takes away the sin of the world"?

A. Mary
B. Isaiah
C. John the Baptist
D. Pilate

4. What was the significance of the number of male goats used for the sin offering during the temple dedication?

A. It represented the number of priests present
B. It symbolized the 12 tribes of Israel
C. It was the number of Levites involved in the offering
D. It was a random number selected by the leaders

5. What was the symbolic meaning of the Passover lamb in the New Testament?

A. It represents the faithfulness of the Israelites
B. It is a symbol of the believer's spiritual renewal
C. It represents Jesus Christ, the Lamb of God who takes away the sins of the world
D. It symbolizes the sacrifice of the firstborn in Egypt

6. The Passover commemorated

A. the coronation of David

B. Cyrus's decree

C. The Jews' freedom from Egypt

D. Israel's first harvest

7. What does the New Testament say about believers being freed from sin?

A. Believers must follow the Law of Moses to be freed from sin

B. Believers are freed from sin by following the teachings of the prophets

C. Believers are freed from sin through the sacrifice of Jesus Christ, the Lamb of God

D. Believers are freed from sin by making sacrifices at the temple

8. How did the people of Israel respond after they repented of their sins?

A. They celebrated with sorrow and mourning

B. They experienced God's restoration and joy

C. They performed additional sacrifices for forgiveness

D. They stopped offering sacrifices and prayed for mercy

9. According to Ezra 6:22, what was the source of the Israelites' joy after the dedication of the temple?

A. God gave them joy after they obeyed His commands

B. They were joyful because they had conquered their enemies

C. They were happy about their political independence

D. They were pleased with the architectural design of the temple

10. How does the Bible portray the role of rulers and kings in relation to God's will?

A. Rulers are beyond God's control and act independently

B. God can influence and direct the hearts of kings to fulfill His purposes

C. Rulers are meant to act only according to the wishes of their people

D. Kings should ignore God's will and focus on personal ambition

What Do You Say?

What is the result of living in obedience to God?

LESSON 4

Ezra Returns from Captivity

Ezra 7—8

Introduction

The situation in Jerusalem and Judah was looking good. The Jews had returned home after 70 years in captivity, the temple had been rebuilt, the priests and Levites were performing their duties. Sacrifices and offerings resumed, and the people observed the Passover and Feast of Unleavened Bread. However, one thing was lacking. The people needed to learn what the Law of Moses required of them. In His grace and mercy, God met that need by sending the scribe Ezra from Babylon to Jerusalem. He would teach the people what they needed to know and do.

Ezra leads a return to Jerusalem (7:1–10)

In the reign of Artaxerxes (465-424 B.C.), Ezra led a second return of exiles to Jerusalem. He was a descendant of Israel's first high priest (7:1–5). He was also a scribe (teacher) who was thoroughly acquainted with the Law of Moses. Not only was he an excellent student of the Law of Moses, but also he was a highly capable teacher of it. He was in good favor with King Artaxerxes, who gave him all he asked for. However, the main reason the king gave him everything he asked for was God's hand was on him. So, Ezra enjoyed both the favor of an earthly king and that favor of God, the almighty King of heaven and earth (7:6).

Accompanying Ezra on his journey to Jerusalem were some exiles, some priests, Levites, singers, and gatekeepers (7:7). It took 4 months to complete the 900-mile journey, according to 7:8, 9). And from start to finish, God's good hand was on him (7:9), because Ezra devoted himself to the study of the Law of Moses (7:10).

Ezra had committed himself to do three things:

1. study the Law of Moses
2. do the Law of Moses
3. teach its statutes and rules in Israel

We are priests and Kings to God in Christ (Revelation 1:6) Just as Ezra purposed, Christians should maintain a similar relationship with God's Word. They need to study it. 2 Timothy 2:15 tells us we need to be unashamed workers who rightly handle the word of truth. They need to do it. Colossians 3:16 says, "Let the word of Christ dwell in you richly." James 1:22 counsels us to "be doers of the word, and not hearers only." They need to share it. Mark 16:15 commands us to "proclaim the gospel to the whole creation."

Artaxerxes gives Ezra an authoritative letter (7:11–26)

Artaxerxes gave Ezra a copy of his letter to carry with him to Jerusalem. It falls into three parts: (1) concerning Ezra (7:11–20), (2) concerning the treasurers beyond the Euphrates (7:21–24), and (3) concerning the appointment of magistrates and judges (7:25, 26).

Ezra, who received the letter from Artaxerxes, is called "the priest, the scribe, a man learned in matters of the commandments of the Lord and his statutes for Israel" (7:11). Quite a compliment from a pagan king! As a priest, Ezra was qualified to offer sacrifices on behalf of the people of Israel, and as a scribe, he was qualified to teach the Scriptures that existed in his day. Artaxerxes granted permission for all who wanted to go to Jerusalem with Ezra to accompany him (7:13). The king and his seven nobles charged Ezra with the responsibility to investigate whether the returnees in Jerusalem and Judah were complying with God's law (7:14). They also charged him with the task of carrying the silver and gold that they had offered to Israel's God (7:15).

Furthermore, they entrusted Ezra with the task of carrying all the silver and gold the king's people in Babylonia had given for offerings in Jerusalem. Apparently, Artaxerxes and his subjects had developed a high regard for the God of Israel, but we should not assume that they had become believers in Him as the only, true God. Ezra was supposed to use the money to buy sacrificial animals, grain offerings, and drink offerings, all of which were to be offered on the temple's altar (7:17). Ezra could use any remaining money as he believed God wanted him to use it (7:18). He was also supposed to carry vessels to Jerusalem to be used in the temple (7:19). If Ezra needed anything else for the temple, he could dip into the king's treasury (7:20).

Artaxerxes' letter also addressed the treasurers in Babylonia and ordered them to supply whatever Ezra required of them, and they were told to do so speedily (7:21). A limit was set on everything except salt (7:22). The limits were 100 silver talents (about 3 tons), 100 cors of wheat (600 bushels), 100 baths of wine (600 gallons), and 100 baths of oil (olive oil). These supplies would be used for grain offerings and drink offerings. Artaxerxes hoped these supplies would persuade God to withhold His wrath from Persia (7:23). Finally, Artaxerxes ordered his subjects not to impose taxes on the temple workers (7:24).

Artaxerxes' letter closed with a couple of instructions for Ezra. Trusting Ezra to exercise God's wisdom, Artaxerxes told him to appoint civil authorities in Jerusalem and Judah. They were supposed to judge those who knew God's laws, and Ezra was supposed to teach God's laws to those who didn't know them (7:25). Speedy judgment was prescribed for those who broke God's laws. It could be execution, banishment, confiscation of goods, or imprisonment (7:26).

Ezra gives thanks (7:27, 28)

With a grateful heart Ezra praised God for persuading Artaxerxes to beautify the temple (7:27). He also thanked Him for manifesting His love to him in the sight of the king, his nobles, and his officers. This divine favor encouraged Ezra. He knew God's hand was on him, so he gathered key men of Israel to journey with him to Jerusalem (7:28).

God prepared Ezra for just this time and purpose, and it was exciting for Him to be part of God's plan. If you are a Christian, God saved you for a purpose. If you do what He wants you to do, His hand will be on you, and you will succeed at doing His will. If you are not a Christian, trust in Jesus as your Savior, and your life will take on significant purpose.

Families who returned with Ezra (8:1–14)

True to his vocation as a scribe, Ezra recorded the names of the heads of families and the numbers of those who made the journey with them (8:1–14). Estimating the number of women and children, the total number of returnees with Ezra may have been between 6,000 and 7,000. This was a much smaller group than the group of 42,360 that Zerubbabel led.

A river rest area (8:15–30)

Travel in Ezra's day was tiring and difficult, especially over the dry, hot terrain between Babylon and Jerusalem. We can only wonder if the children in Ezra's group kept asking, "Are we there yet?" At any rate, Ezra and his people camped for three days at the river Ahava that may have been a tributary of the Euphrates River (8:21). From there, Ezra dispatched a delegation of eleven men to Casiphia (unknown location) to find Levites and temple servants for service in the temple in Jerusalem (8:16, 17). The mission was successful because God's hand was on the delegation, and they brought to Ezra 38 Levites and 220 temple servants to assist the Levites (8:18–20).

Before continuing on the journey to Jerusalem, Ezra held a fast in order for everyone to humble himself before God and ask for a safe journey for everyone and all their goods (8:21). This was a tremendous act of faith, given all the wealth and the small group that they had traveling with it. He had not asked the king for an armed escort for protection, because he had told Artaxerxes that God would take care of the travelers (8:22). Ezra testified that God answered the prayer for safety (8:23). It is appropriate for us to ask God for safety when we begin a journey. He listens and He answers us.

After fasting and praying, Ezra committed what Artaxerxes and his nobles and the Jews in Babylon had offered for the temple (8:24, 25). Ezra listed the inventory (8:26, 27) and told the men that they were holy, and the inventory was holy too. They were responsible to guard the inventory until they turned it over to the priests, the Levites, and the elders in Jerusalem (8:28, 29). The appointed guards of the inventory accepted the responsibility (8:30). Churches, too, are responsible to be good stewards of what is given and safeguard it (see 1 Corinthians 14:40; 2 Corinthians 8:16–24).

The journey from Ahava to Jerusalem (8:31-36)

Ezra and his group arrived in Jerusalem, and on the fourth day delivered the valuable inventory to the temple's officers (8:31–34). Everything was counted and weighed and recorded (8:34).

Next, the returnees from Babylon offered burnt offerings to the Lord: 12 bulls (one for each of the 12 tribes of Israel), 96 rams, 77 lambs, and 12 male goats as a sin offering (8:35) Finally, they gave a copy of Artaxerxes' decree to the neighboring Gentile officials, and in turn the officials helped the returnees in some ways and also helped the temple, likely by contributing sacrificial animals (8:36).

LESSON 4 EXAM

Use the answer sheet that has been provided to complete your exam.

1. What was the main reason Artaxerxes granted Ezra everything he asked for?

A. Ezra's wisdom in governing
B. Artaxerxes' respect for the God of Israel
C. Artaxerxes' desire to expand his empire
D. Ezra's personal wealth and influence

2. Which of the following was NOT one of Ezra's three commitments?

A. Study the Law of Moses
B. Teach the Law of Moses
C. Enforce the Law of Moses
D. Do the Law of Moses

3. Who did Ezra take with him on the journey to Jerusalem?

A. Only the priests
B. Priests, Levites, singers, and gatekeepers
C. A group of soldiers for protection
D. Only wealthy Jewish families

4. How long did it take Ezra's group to travel from Babylon to Jerusalem?

A. 3 months
B. 6 months
C. 4 months
D. 9 months

5. What was Artaxerxes' letter to Ezra primarily concerned with?

A. Ordering military assistance for Ezra's journey
B. Granting financial aid for the rebuilding of the temple
C. Giving authority to Ezra to investigate the observance of God's law in Judah
D. Sending an army to protect the Israelites from attack

6. What specific task did Ezra have with the silver and gold Artaxerxes provided?

A. Use it to buy sacrificial animals, grain offerings, and drink offerings
B. Use it to purchase weapons for defense
C. Use it to pay the workers rebuilding the temple
D. Use it to pay for the journey back to Babylon

7. What did Artaxerxes hope to achieve by supplying these offerings?

A. To make Israel loyal to Persia
B. To ensure the peace between Persia and Israel
C. To persuade God to withhold His wrath from Persia
D. To get political influence in Israel

8. How did Ezra prepare his group for the journey to Jerusalem?

A. He prayed and asked for protection
B. He held a feast for everyone
C. He declared a fast to humble themselves before God and ask for safety
D. He hired an armed escort for the journey

9. What was the main reason Ezra did not request military protection from Artaxerxes?

A. He trusted in the wealth of the group for protection
B. He believed God would take care of the travelers
C. He had enough soldiers among the returnees
D. He wanted to prove that God was with them

10. What did Ezra do when they arrived in Jerusalem with the valuable offerings?

A. He immediately began the construction of the temple
B. He sent the offerings directly to the priests for use in sacrifices
C. He held a public feast to celebrate
D. He counted, weighed, and recorded the offerings

What Do You Say?

What might it look like for us to “study,” “do,” and “teach” God’s Word in practical terms?

____

____

____

____

LESSON 5

Sin and Confession

Ezra 9—10

Introduction

When Ezra arrived in Jerusalem, he found that many of the men, including the priests and the Levites, had married foreign women. They must have forgotten what happened when King Solomon married foreign wives. 1 Kings 11:4 says, "his wives turned away his heart after other gods." Consequently, the Lord told him He would tear the kingdom from him (11:11). Then, too, they must have forgotten what happened four centuries earlier, when Ahab married wicked Jezebel, the daughter of the king of the Sidonians. The marriage was supposed to form a peaceful alliance between Israel and the Phoenicians, but it brought only trouble to Israel. Ahab and Jezebel made Baal worship Israel's official religion. 1 Kings 16:30 says Ahab "did evil in the sight of the Lord, more than all [the kings] who were before him." Because of Ahab's idolatry, the Lord withheld rain from Israel for three and a half years (1 Kings 17:1; James 5:17). The people of Jerusalem and Judah must have forgotten, too, that the worship of false gods was a sin that brought the Babylonian invasion upon them (2 Chronicles 36:14–17).

An appalling situation (9:1–4)

What should have been a joyful arrival in Jerusalem for Ezra was instead an extremely sad event. A report that Ezra received from Israel's officials indicated that the people—even the priests and Levites—had married their pagan neighbors contrary to what was forbidden in Exodus 34:11–16. Consequently, the unholy alliance had caused the guilty Jews to practice pagan abominations (9:1–3). Upon hearing this alarming news, Ezra grieved severely. He tore his clothes, yanked hair from his head and beard, and slumped down utterly appalled (9:4). This was the typical response of godly men when they heard about sin.

Christians, too, are warned not to be unequally yoked with unbelievers. While traditionally interpreted as a warning about marriage to unbelieving spouses, Christians should avoid any alliance that might cause them to sever close fellowship with God and engage in sinful practices (see 2 Corinthians 6:14–18). We must never accept a sin as a necessary evil or soon it will seem more necessary and less evil.

Ezra's prayer of confession (9:5-15)

At the time of the evening sacrifice (3:00 p.m.), Ezra fell on his knees and spread out his hands toward the Lord (9:5). He prayed and identified with the guilty lawbreakers, although he hadn't committed the sin that caused such grief. He referred to "our guilt" and "our iniquities" (9:6). He recalled how Israel's past sins had brought about disasters, including captivity (9:7). But he also mentioned that the Lord had shown grace and love to Israel by influencing the Persian kings to allow His people to return to Jerusalem to rebuild the temple, to restore its ruins, and enjoy the Lord's protection (9:8, 9).

Confessing corporate sins while asking for restoration is a common practice for those close to the Lord. Moses, Israel's great lawgiver and the man God used to lead His enslaved people out of Egypt, identified with Israel's sin. While he was on Mount Sinai receiving instructions from God, the Israelites grew tired of waiting for him. They demanded that Aaron, Moses' brother, make gods for them to worship (Exodus 32:1). Then he made a golden calf that they worshiped and sacrificed to (32:2–6). The Lord told Moses what had happened and that He was going to destroy the nation (32:7–10). But Moses prayed for the people, confessed their sin, and even identified with them. He asked the Lord to forgive them, but added, "But if not, please blot me out of your book that you have written" (32:32).

When the prophet Daniel was in exile in Babylon, he, too, identified with Israel's sins and prayed for forgiveness (Daniel 9:1–19). He did not ask the Lord to forgive Israel's sins because Israel was righteous but because God was so merciful (9:18). When we pray that the Lord will forgive others, we should examine our own lives and confess whatever sins we have committed.

Ezra admitted in his prayer of confession that in spite of God's warnings about marrying their pagan neighbors, the people of Israel had refused the warnings (Ezra 9:10–12). However, Ezra noted that God had punished His sinning people less than they deserved and had left a remnant of His people (9:13). He concluded his confession by admitting that Israel had broken God's commandments by intermarrying pagans and deserved His anger and annihilation (9:14). He also recognized that God is just and had allowed a remnant to return from captivity. Now, that remnant was guilty in His sight (9:15).

The book of Ezra is not suggesting that Gentiles are evil and the Jews are less inherently sinful. The book of Romans opens with three chapters that describe both Jews and Gentiles as sinners. Romans 3:9 announces that "both Jews and Gentiles are under sin." And Romans 3:23 declares that "All have sinned and fall short of the glory of God." The bad news gets worse in Romans 6:23. This verse proclaims that "the wages of sin is death." But the same verse presents the good news that "the free gift of God is eternal life in Christ Jesus our Lord."

God had commanded that the Jews not intermarry with Gentiles, and Ezra knew that his people deserved God's punishment for breaking that command, but he also cast himself and the nation on God's undeserved favor and forgiveness.

When Solomon dedicated the first temple in Jerusalem, the Lord promised Israel, "If my people who are called by my name humble themselves, and pray, and seek my face and turn from their wicked ways, then I will hear from heaven and will forgive their sin and heal their land" (2 Chronicles 7:14). The Lord kept this promise when Ezra confessed the people's sin.

Perhaps your nation has turned its back on God in spite of all the good things He has done for her? Yet, God's love and mercy are so great that He is willing to forgive if the nation repents and asks for forgiveness. Proverbs 14:34 reminds us that "righteousness exalts a nation, but sin is a reproach to any people." Like Ezra, you can intercede for your country in prayer. Why not make it a daily practice to pray for your nation and at the same time confess and forsake your own sins?

Turning back to God (10:1–44)

Ezra was still confessing Israel's sin in front of the temple when a large crowd of men, women, and children gathered around him. They were weeping tremendously because of the sin of intermarrying (10:1). Shecaniah, a priest, whose name means Jehovah has dealt, spoke up for the crowd (10:2). He confessed that the transgressors had turned their backs on God by marrying foreign women, but he saw a glimmer of hope for the nation (10:2). He suggested that the people of God separate from their pagan wives and their children. This action was to be in accordance with God's law (10:3; see Exodus 34:12–16). This would not be an easy action, but those who trembled at God's commandment would carry it out (Ezra 10:3). However, historical evidence indicates that the men were obligated to ensure their former wives' care.

The men who confessed and forsook their sins give us an important example. When a Christian commits a sin, he can choose to continue in sin or confess the sin and receive God's forgiveness. First John 1:9 promises, "If we confess our sins, he [God] is faithful and just to forgive our sins and to cleanse us from all unrighteousness." It may not be easy to humble oneself and confess his sin, but it is much more painful to continue in sin and come under God's hand of discipline.

Shecaniah urged Ezra to call upon the violators of God's law to separate from their wives. He promised to support him in the task, and he called upon him to be strong (Ezra 10:4). Ezra responded by summoning the leading priests, the Levites, and all Israel to take an oath to do what Shecaniah had suggested (10:5).

Ezra spent the night fasting and grieving at the home of Jehohanan, the high priest's grandson (10:6). A proclamation summoned all the returnees to gather in Jerusalem (10:7). Failure to obey the proclamation carried a penalty of forfeiture of property and of being cut off from the Jews and the temple (10:8).

Complying with the proclamation, the returnees gathered in the square east of the temple, where they heard Ezra pronounce their guilt and his command to confess their sin and divorce their foreign wives (10:9–11). The assembly agreed but requested time to do so and permission to appear before their local elders and judges (10:12–14). Four leaders opposed this plan (10:15), but it was launched, and three months later all the marriages were examined (10:16, 17).

True to his position as a scribe, Ezra reported in detail the names of those who had married foreign wives. Interestingly, Meshullam, one of the four men who opposed the plan to divorce the foreign wives, was guilty of marrying a foreign woman (10:29). Even some priests and Levites were among the guilty parties, along with a temple singer and three gatekeepers (10:18–24). Each priest offered a ram as his sin offering (10:19). Unfortunately, some of the guilty returnees had fathered children (10:44).

Ezra had faithfully carried out his duties, and the book of Ezra ends with a report of the people responding to his ministry by turning back to God. All of us sin and need to be familiar with repenting and coming back to the Lord. But the Lord is gracious, welcoming us back into relationship with Him in spite of our sins. This is the best result of any minister's labors, that men and women would come to the Lord and be freed from their sins! Much more than rebuilding a temple, the book of Ezra is about the restoration of a people to God, and the freedom they gained from the sins that had enslaved them.

LESSON 5 EXAM

Use the answer sheet that has been provided to complete your exam.

1. Why was Ezra grieved upon arriving in Jerusalem?
A. The people rejected the rebuilding of the temple
B. The temple had been destroyed again
C. The people refused to pay their tithes
D. The people had married foreign women, breaking God's commandments

2. Which biblical event is mentioned as a warning against marrying foreign wives?
A. The sin of Adam and Eve
B. The fall of Jericho
C. The Tower of Babel
D. King Solomon's marriages

3. What did Ezra initially do when he heard about the sin of intermarriage?
A. He wrote a letter to the Persian king
B. He tore his clothes, pulled his hair and beard, and sat down appalled
C. He offered a public sacrifice to atone for the people's sins
D. He called for a military intervention

4. In his prayer, what did Ezra acknowledge about God's past dealings with Israel?
A. God had given them victories over all their enemies
B. God had already forgiven them without repentance
C. God had completely forsaken them
D. God had punished them less than they deserved

5. In His mercy God had left __________in Israel.
A. a remnant
B. intact walls
C. cultivated vineyards
D. a righteous king

6. What does 1 John 1:9 promise to those who confess their sins?

A. They will be forgiven and cleansed from unrighteousness

B. They will never face consequences for their actions

C. They will receive material blessings

D. They will instantly be healed from illness

7. What action did Shecaniah suggest for the people to take in response to their sin?

A. To offer sacrifices for forgiveness

B. To separate from their foreign wives

C. To flee the country and start over elsewhere

D. To write a letter of apology to the Persian king

8. What consequence did Ezra mention for those who refused to follow the proclamation?

A. Excommunication from the Jewish community

B. A fine for non-compliance

C. Forfeiture of property and being cut off from the community

D. Banishment to foreign lands

9. What role did Ezra take in the process of repentance and separation?

A. He remained silent, allowing the people to decide for themselves

B. He encouraged people to stay married to their foreign wives

C. He organized the process, leading the people in confession and action

D. He left Jerusalem to avoid conflict

10. What does the book of Ezra ultimately focus on, beyond rebuilding the temple?

A. The restoration of political power in Israel

B. The rebuilding of the walls of Jerusalem

C. The restoration of a people's relationship with God

D. The enforcement of strict religious laws

What Do You Say?

Given the example of Ezra and the men of Israel, how should we respond to sin (both our own and that of others)?

LESSON 6

The Power of Prayer

Nehemiah 1:1—2:8

Introduction

How powerful is prayer? The apostle James wrote, "The prayer of a righteous person has great power as it is working" (James 5:16). This truth was evident in the life of Nehemiah. As you will see in this lesson, he offered a quick prayer to the God of heaven that changed the course of history for the Jews who had returned to Jerusalem.

A disturbing report (Nehemiah 1:1–3)

Nehemiah, whose name means the Lord comforts, was in Susa, the winter palace, in Chislev (November-December) in the twentieth year of King Artaxerxes' reign. At that time, he received a delegation of Jews from Judah. When he asked the delegation how the returnees and Jerusalem were doing, they said the returnees were in great trouble and shame. Furthermore, they reported that Jerusalem's walls were broken down and the city's gates were burned to the ground.

Nehemiah prayed (1:4–11)

The disturbing report caused Nehemiah to weep and mourn for days. He also fasted and prayed (1:4). When a nation is in decline or in a weakened condition, its citizens should feel sad but pray to the God of heaven. Nehemiah addressed God as the great and awesome God who faithfully abides by His promises and His unfailing love with those who love and obey Him (1:5).

Nehemiah urged God to answer his prayer. He prayed day and night for the people of Israel and, like Ezra, identified his sins with theirs as he confessed the nation's sins (1:6). He described the sinning as very corrupt, and a violation of the commandments God had given to Moses (1:7). Read Exodus 20:3–17 for a list of the Ten Commandments God gave to Israel.

We can follow Nehemiah's example by praying for others, including our government leaders. We should ask the Lord to bring them to a knowledge of Himself (1 Timothy 2:1–4).

God had promised to scatter His people among the Gentiles if they disobeyed Him but bring them home if they returned to Him and obeyed Him (Nehemiah 1:8, 9). Nehemiah closed his prayer by recalling that the Jews were God's redeemed people and by asking to give him favor in the sight of the king (1:10, 11). He identified himself as the king's cupbearer.

The role of a king's cupbearer was extremely risky. It was similar to that of a security guard for a head of state. The guards must be willing to stand between an assassin's bullet and the head of state. Similarly, a cupbearer stood between a would-be assassin's poison and the king. The cupbearer would taste food and drink before it reached the king. If the food or drink was poisoned, the cupbearer would drop dead, but the king's life would be spared. It's not surprising that a king often appreciated his cupbearer and considered him an important official in his royal court.

Nehemiah's double risk (2:1-3)

In March–April of the of King Artaxerxes' reign, Nehemiah was still grieving over the plight of Jerusalem the city he loved. Wine was delivered to the king, and faithful to his position as cupbearer, Nehemiah sampled the wine and handed it to Artaxerxes. This was the first risk Nehemiah took that day. The second risk was his looking sad. Any servant in the royal court could forfeit his position by looking unhappy in the king's presence. Looking sad might even result in the death penalty.

Artaxerxes discerned that Nehemiah wasn't sick but was sad. When he mentioned Nehemiah's sadness, Nehemiah was "very much afraid" (2:2).

Would he be banished from the royal court? Would he be executed? He had good reason to be afraid.

Nehemiah answered the king. First, he wished the king a long life. He explained that he was sad because Jerusalem, where his ancestors were buried, was in ruins and its gates were burned to the ground (2:3).

Nehemiah's silent prayer (2:4)

Instead of penalizing Nehemiah, Artaxerxes asked what he was requesting. Before telling the king what his request was, Nehemiah prayed to the God of heaven (2:4). That's it. We don't have any specific words that Nehemiah prayed, but that isn't what's important. Presumably while standing in front of the king, Nehemiah took just a moment to pray to King of Kings. The title, "God of heaven," portrays Him as sovereign, in full control of everything and everyone. Nehemiah stood in the presence of a powerful king, but he was aware of the ability of the all-powerful King of heaven and earth to answer his prayer.

Many people are concerned with having just the right words in a prayer. The Bible makes it clear that God is not impressed with long, high-sounding prayers. A simple prayer offered in faith pleases Him and gets results. Jesus said, "And when you pray, do not heap up empty phrases as the Gentiles do, for they think that they will be heard for their many words" (Matthew 6:7). He said, "Ask, and it will be given to you" (7:7).

Peter serves as an example of someone who offered a short but urgent prayer to the Lord in a perilous situation. He was sinking in the Sea of Galilee with the wind howling around him, and he cried out to the Lord, "Lord, save me" (Matthew 14:30). Jesus answered Peter's brief prayer for help (14:31).

Jesus told a parable (a story that presents a spiritual truth) about a hypocritical Pharisee and a tax collector. The two men prayed in the temple. The Pharisee boasted to God on and on about his religious practices (Luke 18:11, 12), but the tax collector simply prayed, "God, be merciful to me a sinner" (18:13). Jesus said the humble tax collector went home in a right relationship with God (18:14).

When Jesus was on the cross along with two criminals, one criminal insulted Him (Luke 23:39), but the other criminal turned to Him in repentance, and cried out, "Jesus, remember me when you come into your kingdom" (23:42). Jesus answered this short prayer by promising the repentant criminal, "Truly, I say to you, today you will be with me in paradise" (23:43).

You don't have to be an eloquent theologian to pray; simply tell the Lord in simple words what you need. If you need forgiveness, simply ask

Him to forgive you and give you a new life. Romans 10:13 promises, "Everyone who calls on the name of the Lord will be saved."

Nehemiah's quick silent prayer brought favorable results.

Nehemiah's request to the king (2:5–8)

Phrased in respectful words, Nehemiah asked for permission to return to Jerusalem to rebuild it (2:5). Would the king grant Nehemiah's bold request? With the queen sitting beside him, would it make him look weak in her eyes to do what his servant, a cupbearer, asked? He withheld his answer until he asked and received Nehemiah's answer to the question, "How long will you be gone, and when will you return?" Apparently, pleased with Nehemiah's response, the king granted Nehemiah permission to return to Jerusalem (2:6).

Nehemiah knew he would receive opposition to his venture from the nations that occupied the region between Persia and Judah. So, he boldly but politely asked the king for letters addressed to the various governors advising them to give Nehemiah safe passage (2:7). He even asked for a letter to the keeper of the king's forest. The letter would request timber with which Nehemiah would build the gates of the citadel that protected the temple (2:8). He also needed timber for the rebuilding of the walls and for the construction of his own house (2:8). He sent a requisition to the man who was in charge of the king's forest, Asaph.

Was Artaxerxes weary of all Nehemiah's requests? Not at all, he granted all of the requests, because God's good hand was upon Nehemiah (2:8). When God guides His obedient children, He accomplishes His will. No one and nothing can disrupt His plan!

LESSON 6 EXAM

Use the answer sheet that has been provided to complete your exam.

1. Who was the King of Persia when Nehemiah served in the palace?

A. Cyrus
B. Nebuchadnezzar
C. Darius
D. Artaxerxes

2. How did Nehemiah react when he heard about the troubles in Jerusalem?

A. He ignored it and continued his duties
B. He wrote a letter to the king
C. He wept, mourned, fasted, and prayed
D. He immediately traveled to Jerusalem

3. What does the name Nehemiah mean?

A. The Lord reigns
B. The Lord comforts
C. The Lord understands
D. The Lord answers prayer

4. What position did Nehemiah hold in the Persian court?

A. Governor
B. King's cupbearer
C. High priest
D. Royal architect

5. Why did Nehemiah fear for his life when the king noticed his sadness?

A. The king could have thought Nehemiah was plotting against him
B. A servant could be punished or executed for appearing sad in the king's presence
C. Nehemiah had fallen out of favor with the king
D. He feared his request would be rejected

6. What did Nehemiah do before making his request to King Artaxerxes?

A. He made a long speech explaining the situation
B. He waited for a dream to direct him
C. He consulted with his fellow servants
D. He prayed silently to the God of heaven

7. What request did Nehemiah make of King Artaxerxes?

A. To return to Jerusalem and rebuild the city
B. To be released from his position as cupbearer
C. To send soldiers to defend Jerusalem
D. To grant him permission to marry the queen

8. What additional request did Nehemiah make to King Artaxerxes?

A. A letter to the governors of the region for safe passage
B. A large monetary donation for the rebuilding
C. Permission to hire workers from other regions
D. Permission to relocate his family to Jerusalem

9. How did King Artaxerxes respond to Nehemiah's requests?

A. He refused Nehemiah's request and dismissed him
B. He granted all of Nehemiah's requests
C. He demanded that Nehemiah stay in Persia
D. He ordered Nehemiah to take a census of Jerusalem first

10. What is one lesson we can learn from Nehemiah's approach to prayer?

A. Prayers must be long and eloquent to be effective
B. Only the especially righteous can expect answers to their prayers
C. Simple, heartfelt prayers offered in faith are powerful
D. Prayer is only effective when it is offered publicly

What Do You Say?

In times of crisis or distress, how do we typically respond?

____

____

____

____

LESSON 7

No Situation Is Too Hard for God to Handle

Nehemiah 2:9–20

Introduction

Building walls in the ancient world was an incredible task and full of peril. The Great Wall of China was not built to attract tourists, but to keep invaders out of the Chinese Empire. It took 2,000 years to build the 13,000-mile wall, and it cost 400,000 builders their lives. Allegedly, those workers are buried inside the wall. The building of the 73-mile Hadrian's Wall began in A.D.122 in England, and it took 8,000 workers six years to complete it. It, too, was constructed as a defensive barrier.

Nehemiah returned to Jerusalem to rebuild Jerusalem's wall that was destroyed by the Babylonians. The wall was about two miles long and had ten gates and about eight towers. The former cupbearer faced a monumental task. But no matter what the difficulty, be it building giant walls in the past or our own greatest challenges today, no situation is too hard for God to handle.

An unwelcome arrival (2:9, 10)

Nehemiah arrived in Judah and gave the provincial governors west of the Euphrates the letters from Artaxerxes that demanded Nehemiah's safe passage. Of course, the military escort Artaxerxes had provided must have helped to guarantee safe passage (2:9). Two men, perhaps governors of Samaria and Ammon, were extremely upset by Nehemiah's safe arrival. They hated to see him arrive to help the Jews (2:10).

Did Nehemiah's arrival come before, after, or at the same time as Ezra's arrival? It seems that it came 13 to 14 years after Ezra's arrival. Ezra returned around 458 B.C., and Nehemiah returned around 445 B.C.

Nehemiah views the walls (2:11-16)

Nehemiah stayed in Jerusalem for three days before inspecting the city's walls (2:11). We can only guess what he was doing in those three days. We know he wasn't telling everyone about his mission to repair the walls, but he shared it with a few men (2:12). Perhaps he fasted and prayed for three days. It is always wise to pray before taking on a task you believe God wants you to do.

After three days, Nehemiah arose during the night, and riding a horse, mule, or donkey, he began to inspect the walls (2:12, 13). This was a wise move. It is important to gather prudent information when possible as we seek to do what God wants us to do. Jesus approved of this step. He asked, "For which of you, desiring to build a tower, does not first sit down and count the cost, whether he has enough to complete it?" (Luke 14:28). When accepting the challenge to do what God wants you to do, do not gloss over the difficulty. Consider the difficulties you will encounter. Nehemiah saw that Jerusalem's walls were broken down and its gates had been destroyed by fire (2:13).

Nehemiah began his nighttime inspection at the Valley Gate in the southwest wall. Then he proceeded to the Dragon Spring (an unknown site) and then to the Dung Gate in the southeast section of Jerusalem (2:13). From there, he proceeded to the Fountain Gate on the eastern wall. When he reached the King's Pool, perhaps known later as the Pool of Siloam, the debris was so dense that he could not ride past it (2:14). Then he rode to a valley, likely east of Jerusalem, and back to the city by way of the Valley Gate (2:15).

No one knew where Nehemiah had been or what his mission was until he told them (2:16). Ecclesiastes 3:7 tells us there is "a time to keep silence and a time to speak." Nehemiah was well aware of these times.

God equips the called

Rebuilding the walls would be a daunting project. Archaeologists report that the walls were 39 feet tall, 8 feet wide, and two miles long. Furthermore, Nehemiah had been a cupbearer, not a builder. Nevertheless, he believed it was God's will to rebuild the walls, and therefore He would supply all that was needed to succeed. Like Nehemiah, we can succeed in whatever God calls us to do. His call guarantees His supply of all that we need. Over and over again, Scripture shows us how God equips those He calls to do the tasks He calls them to.

Noah wasn't a carpenter, nor had he ever seen a boat or rain. Yet, when the Lord told him to build the ark, he obeyed. The Lord gave him detailed instructions for building the ark, and when it was built, He brought Noah, his family, and a variety of animals and birds into the ark. Then He closed the door. Fountains of the deep erupted and rain cascaded down from heaven. Every living thing outside the ark perished, but every passenger inside the ark survived. (See Genesis 6:9—8:19.)

Gideon wasn't a warrior. He was a farmer, but the Lord called him to defeat the hordes of Midianite invaders. At first, Gideon told the Lord he was the least in his father's house, but the Lord used him and 300 men with trumpets and jars to defeat the vast Midianite army. (See Judges 6:11—7:25.)

David wasn't a warrior. He was a shepherd boy, but the Lord used him to slay the Philistine giant Goliath, who taunted the army of Israel. And he did it with a well-aimed stone from his slingshot. He relied on the Lord for the victory, and the Lord made him victorious. When David approached Goliath, he cried out, "You come to me with a sword and with a spear and a javelin, but I come to you in the name of the LORD of hosts, the God of the armies of Israel This day the LORD will deliver you into my hand, and I will strike you down and cut off your head" (1 Samuel 17:45, 46).

Peter, Andrew, James, and John had fished all night but had caught nothing. They were washing their empty nets, when the Lord stepped into the scene and commanded them to row out into deep water and let down their nets. Peter told Jesus they had fished all night but had caught nothing. However, he said he would do what Jesus commanded. When the fishermen obeyed Jesus, their nets filled with so many fish that they began to break (see Luke 5:1–7).

In all of these situations, Scripture shows us that it is always best to obey the Lord and leave the results to Him. He never makes a mistake. Psalm 18:30 assures us that God's way is perfect.

Do not fear what man can do to you (2:17–20)

Believing that the Lord would bless the rebuilding of Jerusalem's ruined walls, Nehemiah urged the assembled group to recognize the fact that Jerusalem was in ruins and its gates were burned, but he said "Come, let us build the wall of Jerusalem, that we may no longer suffer derision" (Nehemiah 2:17).

Nehemiah didn't sugarcoat the situation, nor did he communicate despair. A good leader is truthful. He doesn't pretend that everything is rosy. He describes every situation as it is, regardless of how difficult or dangerous it may be. However, he also speaks optimistically because God is present, and He is good. Nehemiah told the group that the hand of God had been upon him, and the King of Persia supported the building project (2:18).

Jesus assured His followers that they would have tribulation in the world, but He also told them to take heart because He had overcome the world (John 16:33). He never hid His scars when he summoned His followers to take the gospel to the ends of the earth.

So, Christians are both pessimistic and optimistic. They see the world as it is, evil and under the sway of the Devil (1 John 5:19). But they also believe that "everyone who has been born of God overcomes the world" (5:4).

Those who accepted Nehemiah's challenge to rebuild Jerusalem's walls said, "Let us rise up and build" (Nehemiah 2:18). But there was a contrasting response. Sanballat, Tobiah, and Geshem jeered at the Jews who were committed to the task of rebuilding the walls. They accused them of rebelling against the King of Persia (2:19).

Nehemiah didn't cave into their insults and accusations. Instead, he told the enemies that the God of heaven would make His servants successful. He also told them they had no "portion or right or claim in Jerusalem" (2:20).

If you believe God has called upon you to serve Him, don't let rough circumstances or scoffers sidetrack you. God will not fail you, so full speed ahead!

LESSON 7 EXAM

Use the answer sheet that has been provided to complete your exam.

1. Why were the provincial governors upset about Nehemiah's arrival?
A. They were jealous of Nehemiah's authority
B. They disagreed with King Artaxerxes' decision
C. They feared Nehemiah's military power
D. They hated to see Nehemiah come to help the Jews

2. How long did Nehemiah stay in Jerusalem before inspecting the city's walls?
A. 1 day
B. 3 days
C. 7 days
D. 14 days

3. What was the reason Nehemiah did not tell everyone about his mission immediately?
A. He was still unsure of his plans
B. He wanted to avoid opposition
C. He was waiting for divine instruction
D. He wanted to gather information first

4. What was Nehemiah's main message to the people of Jerusalem when he gathered them together?
A. To remain silent and pray for deliverance
B. To abandon the project and seek peace
C. To rebuild the walls of Jerusalem to end their shame
D. To seek permission from the king before starting the work

5. What did Nehemiah believe would make the rebuilding of the walls successful?
A. The people's strength and unity
B. The financial support of the king
C. The hand of God being upon him
D. The military protection of Artaxerxes

6. How did Nehemiah respond to the accusations from his enemies?

A. He ignored them

B. He defended himself to the king

C. He told them that the God of heaven would give success

D. He fled Jerusalem

7. What was the response of the people when Nehemiah shared his plan to rebuild the walls?

A. They were afraid and refused to help

B. They asked for a detailed plan

C. They said, "Let us rise up and build"

D. They doubted Nehemiah's ability

8. What does Nehemiah's action of inspecting the walls at night teach us about leadership?

A. Leadership is about being secretive

B. Leaders should avoid difficult tasks

C. Leaders should rely only on others' reports

D. Good leaders gather information and assess situations carefully

9. What lesson can we learn from the story of Nehemiah and the rebuilding of the walls?

A. God equips those He calls to accomplish His will

B. Difficult tasks should be avoided at all costs

C. Only professionals can accomplish God's work

D. Leaders should rely on their own strength

10. Nehemiah told his jeering critics that

A. He would not rebuild the walls

B. God would make the builders successful

C. He would fight them

D. they frightened him

What Do You Say?

How can we, as Christians, respond to criticism and opposition when pursuing God's calling for our lives?

LESSON 8

Organized to Rebuild Jerusalem's Walls

Nehemiah 3

Introduction

Can you picture what it would be like if a wealthy person gave someone a massive budget to build a mansion for him, but there was no blueprint? Furthermore, the person in charge of the project hired 30 men to do the work, but didn't assign them to work on specific projects. Likely, the work would not begin, or the workers would be so disorganized that the building project would be disastrous! For any construction job to be successful, there must be a plan, and the workers must be organized. Nehemiah's effort to restore Jerusalem's walls and gates followed a carefully organized plan, and the workers knew precisely what their responsibilities were.

The rebuilding starts (3:1–5)

The first stage of the rebuilding process is identified as the building of Sheep Gate, located at the northeast corner of Jerusalem. The builders were Eliashib, the high priest and his fellow priests. Eliashib was the grandson of the high priest Jeshua, who served during the time of Zerubbabel (see Ezra 3:2). Nehemiah 13:4–9 reveals that later Eliashib did the unspeakable; he provided a room for Tobiah the Ammonite in the court of the temple.

It is appropriate that priests were assigned to the wall by the Sheep Gate, because sheep and other animals were brought through that gate to the temple to be sacrificed. When Eliashib and the other priests had completed the Sheep Gate, they dedicated it and repaired their section of the wall as far as the Tower of the Hundred and the Tower of Hananel (3:1). The precise location of these towers is unknown, but scholars indicate they were between the Sheep Gate and the Fish Gate.

The men of Jericho and Zaccur also participated in the rebuilding of the walls (3:2). This is the first time in Nehemiah 3 that the phrase "next to" appears. The phrases "next to him" and "next to them" appears frequently throughout the chapter and shows how well organized the project was. Each group of builders had specific areas that were their designated responsibility. The building of the Church, the Body of Christ, is also orderly and well organized. Writing to the Corinthians, the apostle Paul points out in 1 Corinthians 12:12: "For just as the body is one and has many members, and all the members, though many, are one, so it is with Christ." He explains in chapter 12 that the Holy Spirit has given gifts to individuals in the Body of Christ (the Church) for its building up (edifying) of the Body (12:4–27; Ephesians 4:11–13).

As a body needs different kinds of members in order to function, so does the church. It is important that each part does its job, as other parts of the body are not suited to do them. We simply cannot see with our ears! Romans 12 highlights many of the distinctive gifts that God gives the members of His church to use in service to Him. If you are a believer, read Romans 12:3–8 to determine which service gift(s) is yours.

Another group of builders, the sons of Hassenaah, constructed the Fish Gate, in the northern section of the wall (3:3). Working next to them was Meremoth, and next to him was Meshullam. Zadok worked next to him These men also repaired a section of the wall (3:4).

The Tekoites from Tekoa, about 12 miles south of Jerusalem, repaired their section of the wall, but their nobles refused to work (3:5). Perhaps they considered such work undignified, or they may have feared reprisals from the neighboring Gentiles. However, the Tekoites accepted another responsibility. They repaired another section of the wall. Nehemiah 3:27 reports that they "repaired another section opposite the great projecting tower as far as the wall of Ophel." Ophel lay between Jerusalem and the temple mount. Just as the Tekoites took on additional work, so some believers take on extra work that others refused to do. It has been said that the Church is full of willing workers. Some are willing to work, and the rest are willing to let them. May this not be the case in our own churches.

The work continues (3:6–32)

While this section may appear to be just a list of names and the areas they worked, there are a number of things we can learn from this portion of Scripture. The Bible makes it clear that a diverse group of workers contributed to the rebuilding of the wall. The workers included priests (3:1, 22, 28), goldsmiths (3:8, 31, 32), makers of perfume (3:8), government officials (3:9–12, 14–19), Levites (3:17), and merchants (3:31, 32). And not all the workers were men. Nehemiah 3:12 reports that a government official's daughters participated in the rebuilding effort.

No Christian is excluded from the privilege of sharing in the Lord's work. Jesus' disciples included fishermen, a tax collector, and a Zealot (a political activist). Later, workers for the Lord included Paul, a Pharisee; Luke, a doctor; Lydia, a businesswoman; Prisca and Aquila, a husband-wife couple; and a number of others (see Romans 16 and Colossians 4:7–17).

Don't assume that you have to be famous or super talented to serve the Lord. He delights in using ordinary people to achieve extraordinary things. First Corinthians 1:26-29 says, "For consider your calling brothers: not many of you were wise according to worldly standards, not many were powerful, not many were of noble birth, but God chose what is foolish in the world to shame the wise; God chose what is weak in the world to shame the strong. God chose what is low and despised in the world, even things that are not, to bring to nothing things that are, so that no human being might boast in the presence of God."

Dwight L. Moody was a shoe store clerk when God saved him, and one day Moody heard a preacher say, "God is yet to see what He can do through a man that is fully dedicated to Him." D. L. Moody responded by saying, "By the grace of God I will be that man." Subsequently, God used Moody to preach on two continents and lead many people to trust in Christ for salvation.

Nehemiah's leadership not only gave different occupations an opportunity to help rebuild the walls, but also, he assigned sections of the wall to people who lived near the wall. (Nehemiah 3:21, 23, 24, 26, 28–30). This was a wise decision. These people would take a special interest in fortifying the sections of the wall that were close to home. Plus, if they were attacked, they would fight hard to protect their respective property.

Repairing the wall and its towers was not easy. It involved heavy lifting. Nehemiah 3:3 tells us the sons of Hassenaah built the Fish Gate and laid its beams and set its doors. Verse 6 reports that Joiada and Meshullam repaired the Gate of Yehanah and "laid its beams and set its doors." This is heavy work!

Similarly, the work of the Lord is still not easy, but it is rewarding. The apostle Paul experienced numerous hardships during his work for the Lord. He described some of his sufferings in 2 Corinthians 11:23–27. He lists imprisonments, countless beatings, near death experiences, thirty-nine lashes five times, three beatings with rods, a stoning, shipwreck, dangers from robbers, danger in the city and in the wilderness, danger at sea, danger of betrayal, sleeplessness, hunger and thirst. Nevertheless, he knew the Lord would reward his efforts (2 Timothy 4:6–8), Furthermore, he challenged all Christians to "be steadfast, immovable, always abounding in the work of the Lord, knowing that in the Lord your labor is not in vain (1 Corinthians 15:58).

Although the builders made good progress in their determination to rebuild the walls that had been ruined by the Babylonians, much work remained to be done.

Nehemiah 3:6–32 mentions the gates that the organized workers rebuilt. They are the Sheep Gate, the Fish Gate, the Gate of Yeshanah (the Old Gate), the Valley Gate, the Dung Gate, the Fountain Gate, the Water Gate, the Horse Gate, and the East Gate. The Sheep Gate was where sheep and other animals passed on their way to the temple to be sacrificed. The Fish Gate may have been where fishermen brought their fish to market. The Old Gate was located in the northwest corner of Jerusalem. The Valley Gate and Dung Gate at the southern end of the city were where refuse was carried to the Valley of Hinnom to be burned. The Fountain Gate was near the Pool of Siloam. The Water Gate was on the east side of the city. The Valley Gate, southwest of the city, is where Nehemiah's inspection began. The Horse Gate was near the temple on the east. Perhaps it was where riders entered the vicinity of the palace. The East Gate, east of the temple, was where Jesus entered Jerusalem and was greeted as Israel's Messiah (Matthew 21:7–9). Each of these was a great labor by the men and women on this list, and they are not forgotten in God's account of history.

LESSON 8 EXAM

Use the answer sheet that has been provided to complete your exam.

1. Who was responsible for the rebuilding of the Sheep Gate?

A. The goldsmiths
B. The priests, led by Eliashib
C. The sons of Hassenaah
D. The Tekoites

2. What role did the phrase "next to him" serve in Nehemiah 3?

A. It indicated the organization and cooperation among workers
B. It emphasized the leaders' positions
C. It referred to the nobles' leadership
D. It described the geographical locations of the gates

3. Who did the Tekoites represent in the rebuilding effort?

A. Wealthy merchants
B. Priests who served at the temple
C. A group of workers who completed their section, despite some nobles refusing to work
D. Officials and leaders from the region

4. What is highlighted about the workers in Nehemiah 3?

A. Only men participated in the work
B. The workers included people from a variety of occupations and backgrounds
C. All workers were from the tribe of Levi
D. Only the wealthy and noble participated in the rebuilding

5. What specific feature of the workers does Nehemiah 3:12 mention?

A. That women also participated in the work
B. That the workers only came from Jerusalem
C. That all workers were skilled craftsmen
D. That there were no volunteers, only paid workers

6. Why did Nehemiah assign people to work near their homes?

A. To prevent them from being attacked by enemies

B. To reduce the cost of transportation

C. To encourage pride in their work

D. To ensure workers were familiar with their areas

7. What is described as a significant part of the rebuilding work in Nehemiah 3?

A. Building gates and setting doors

B. Laying the foundation stones

C. Planting trees around the city

D. Restoring the temple

8. What does Nehemiah 3:3 reveal about the Fish Gate?

A. It was the only gate that was not rebuilt

B. It was the primary gate used for trade

C. It was built by the sons of Hassenaah

D. It was situated in the southern part of the city

9. What can we learn from the work ethic of the Tekoites, who repaired an additional section of the wall?

A. They were hesitant to contribute until they were encouraged

B. Some workers always need to be paid in order to work

C. They took on extra responsibility even when others refused to help

D. They completed their work with little enthusiasm

10. How does the diverse participation in the rebuilding effort reflect the nature of the Church?

A. Only skilled leaders can contribute to God's work

B. Only those with financial resources are called to serve

C. Every believer, regardless of background or occupation, is called to serve

D. Only those who are directly involved in ministry should work for God

What Do You Say?

Nehemiah involved people from all walks of life in the rebuilding project, regardless of their status or skills. How can this encourage us to engage in God's work, regardless of our background or resources?

LESSON 9

Dealing with Ridicule, Hostility, and Domestic Crises

Nehemiah 4—5

Introduction

When the shepherd boy David visited his soldier brothers, he found them and the rest of the army of Israel terrified of the Philistine giant Goliath. Goliath was almost 10 feet tall. He wore a bronze helmet, a coat of armor that weighed about 125 pounds, and bronze leggings. He carried a bronze javelin and a long spear with a tip that weighed 15 pounds. Behind him on the side of a mountain was the Philistine army. The army of Israel was in front of him on the opposite mountain. Goliath stood in the valley and taunted the Israelite army. He challenged the army of Israel to send a man to fight him. The Israelite soldiers and Saul, their king, refused the challenge. First Samuel 17:11 reports that "they were dismayed and greatly afraid."

David, however, took on the challenge, although he was armed with only a staff, a slingshot, and five smooth stones. Goliath jeered at David, but he stopped jeering when David killed him with a well-aimed stone to his forehead. David won the battle because his trust was in God. He knew God was on his side. (For the full account of this event, read 1 Samuel 17.)

Nehemiah, too, faced the insults of a strong enemy with an army behind him. However, also like David, Nehemiah met the enemy with faith and reliance on God. He exercised godly wisdom in not taking matters into his own hands. Instead, he trusted in the Lord.

Nehemiah responds to ridicule (4:1–6)

Nehemiah and his workers were making progress as they built Jerusalem's wall. But Sanballat, a Samaritan, was irate (4:1). He aimed his anger at the builders and ridiculed them. He called them "feeble Jews." (4:2). He wanted to discourage the builders, but also, he may have wanted to appear brave in "the presence of his brothers and of the army of Samaria" (4:2). He realized that the builders would offer sacrifices of thanksgiving upon completion of the wall. He tried to discourage them by making the task of building the wall seem impossible. He suggested that all they had to work with were "burned stones collected from heaps of rubbish" (4:2).

Ridicule is a tool the Devil uses frequently. Our Lord received ridicule at the hands of Pilate's soldiers (Matthew 27:27–31), and passersby and the thieves on the cross ridiculed Him (27:39–44). However, Jesus had predicted this offensive treatment (Luke 18:31–32), and told His followers, "A servant is not greater than his master. If they persecuted me, they will also persecute you" (John 15:20). The apostle Paul, too, was ridiculed when he proclaimed on Mars Hill that Jesus had risen from the dead (Acts 17:32). If you are a Christian, expect to be ridiculed. Jesus told His followers, "A servant is not greater than his master. If they persecuted me, they will also persecute you" (John 15:20). But He also said, "Take heart; I have overcome the world" (16:33).

Tobiah, the Ammonite, was standing beside Sanballat. He joined in the verbal assault on Nehemiah and the builders by ridiculing their work. We should not be surprised to have our work for the Lord criticized. It is a vicious effort to persuade us to stop working for the Lord. Tobiah asked, "What are they building—if a fox goes up on it he will break down their stone wall!" (Nehemiah 4:3). What an insult! Tobiah suggested that by simply climbing on the wall a fox weighing only a few pounds could demolish what the builders had constructed.

Nehemiah didn't argue with Sanballat and Tobiah. Perhaps he recalled the counsel of Proverbs 26:4, "Answer not a fool according to his folly, lest you be like him yourself." Nehemiah turned the matter over to the Lord. He told the Lord he and his workers were despised, and he asked Him to bring disaster on his adversaries and their land. Furthermore, he asked the Lord not to cover their guilt but to blot them out of His sight, because they had angered Him in the builders' presence (Nehemiah 4:4, 5).

Sanballat and Tobiah, backed by the army of Samaria, could not halt the building of the wall. After praying, Nehemiah and the workers went right back to the task at hand. The people were determined to build the wall, and they succeeded at building it to half its intended height (4:6).

Nehemiah responds to hostility (4:7–23)

Sanballat and Tobiah's words had failed to stop the building of the wall, so they resorted to weapons. Enemies from all directions plotted to fight to stop the construction of the wall (4:8). But Nehemiah and the builders prayed and posted a guard day and night (4:9). When trouble threatens us, our first course of action should be prayer. We can do more than pray, but we should not decide what to do without first praying.

In addition to the threat from the enemies, the builders were growing weak and pessimistic (4:10). They also faced a surprise attack (4:11). Plus, the builders' neighbors kept pleading with them to leave the wall and return home to protect their families and property (4:12).

In that dark hour, Nehemiah acted. He stationed guards with swords, spears and bows behind the lowest parts of the wall (4:13), and he told everyone not to fear but to remember that the Lord is great and awesome. He also told them to fight for their families, encouraging them to continue the work (4:14, 15). The work could have been lost due to discouragement, but the workers persevered.

The enemies learned that their plan did not work, and the construction of the wall continued (4:15). Half of the workers built and half of them carried weapons (4:15, 16). Nehemiah continued to encourage the builders by telling them the work they were doing was great, although they were separated from one another on the wall. He gave the order to rush to the part of the wall where the trumpet sounded. He assured everyone that God would fight for them (4:17–20).

While half the workers held weapons, the builders worked around the clock under the watchful eye of guards (4:21–23). Both the carriers of weapons and the builders were used of God to carry out His plan to complete the wall. Christians do not have the same God-given roles, but every role is important, and we can cooperate in the work of the Lord. Like those who watched for the enemy and carried weapons, Christians should watch for the attacks of the Devil (1 Peter 5:8) and resist him and his cohorts. Ephesians 6:11–18 lists the weapons and armor that God has made available to each of us.

So armed, we can "stand" in the evil day against the attacks of the evil one. Taking the sword of the Spirit, the Word of God, is an essential weapon in warding off temptation. Matthew 4 reports that every time the Devil tempted Jesus, He repelled the temptation with a specific word from Deuteronomy. Like the workers who were armed for defense, we can also watch for the attacks of the evil one against our brothers and sisters, praying for them and protecting them from discouragement.

Nehemiah responds to domestic crises (5:1–13)

Trouble doesn't always come from unbelievers like those who opposed the building of the wall. Sometimes it arises from God's people. Nehemiah 5:1 reports an outcry arose among the Jews. It seems the poor people faced a food shortage and could not feed their families (5:2). Likely, threats from Judah's enemies kept many people from working their farms, and a drought had caused a famine (5:3). The landowners had to mortgage their fields, vineyards, and houses to buy grain. Some people complained that they had to borrow money to pay the property tax to the King of Persia (5:4). Ultimately, these people sold their children as slaves to pay their creditors (5:5).

All these complaints severely angered Nehemiah (5:6). He confronted the nobles and officials (the wealthy Jews), accusing them of exacting interest from their fellow Jews. This practice disregarded God's command not to charge fellow Israelites interest (see Exodus 22:25; Leviticus 25:35–38; Deuteronomy 15:7, 8).

Nehemiah called a large assembly and reminded the guilty that he and others had rescued enslaved Jews but now the wealthy Jews were selling fellow Jews into slavery. The guilty Jews had no answer (Nehemiah 5:9). Continuing his indictment, Nehemiah counseled the guilty Jews to live in the fear of God to keep the Gentile enemies from laughing at them (5:9). He pointed out that he and some others were lending the needy grain and money. He called for an end to the practice of charging interest and demanded that the guilty ones return everything they had taken from the poor (5:10, 11). Finally, he received an answer. Those guilty of wrongdoing agreed to do what Nehemiah said (5:12). Nehemiah held them to their promise by requiring them to take an oath. In a symbolic act, he shook out the fold of his garment and implored God to shake out every promise breaker from his house and possessions. The assembly agreed and praised the Lord; and "the people did as they had promised" (5:13).

Nehemiah's generosity (5:14-19)

Nehemiah 5:14–18 describes Nehemiah's extreme generosity. He practiced what he preached. During his 12 years as Judah's governor, he declined a food allowance. The former governors had charged the people about a pound of silver and a food allowance, but to the contrary, Nehemiah supplied free meals for 150 Jews, officials, and guests from the surrounding nations. This daily generosity required the purchase of an ox, six sheep, and poultry, but he did not ask for a governor's food allowance.

As was Nehemiah's frequent habit, he followed the description of his generosity with prayer. He asked his God to remember what he had done for the people of Judah (5:19).

LESSON 9 EXAM

Use the answer sheet that has been provided to complete your exam.

1. What was the first response of Nehemiah when faced with ridicule from Sanballat and Tobiah?

A. He argued with them publicly
B. He ignored them and continued his work
C. He prayed and turned the situation over to God
D. He threatened to stop the work

2. What did Tobiah the Ammonite say about the wall Nehemiah and his workers were building?

A. "A fox could break it down"
B. "The wall will be finished in no time"
C. "The wall will be impenetrable"
D. "The wall will protect us from all enemies"

3. What action did Nehemiah take to prepare for a possible attack on the wall builders?

A. He abandoned the project
B. He stationed guards with swords, spears, and bows
C. He sent the workers home to protect their families
D. He retaliated against the attackers immediately

4. What did Nehemiah encourage the workers to remember when fear and discouragement set in?

A. Their personal safety
B. That the task would be easier if they worked together
C. That the Lord is great and awesome
D. That they had already completed half of the wall

5. What was Nehemiah's strategy to ensure both construction and defense continued simultaneously?

A. Half the workers built while half guarded with weapons
B. Everyone worked together on the wall, with no one guarding
C. Workers took turns guarding the city gates
D. All workers left the wall and retreated to their homes

6. How did Nehemiah address the domestic crisis among the people in Nehemiah 5?

A. He ignored the complaints and focused on the wall

B. He prayed for God to provide food and shelter

C. He told the people to leave the work and return to their farms

D. He confronted the wealthy nobles and officials for exploiting the poor

7. What did Nehemiah demand from the wealthy Jews who had been charging interest?

A. That they build the wall to repay their debts

B. That they apologize publicly and return what was taken from the poor

C. That they stop lending money to anyone

D. That they donate food to the poor

8. How did Nehemiah ensure the wealthy Jews kept their promise to repay what they had taken from the poor?

A. He had them sign a formal contract

B. He shook out the fold of his garment and prayed that God would shake out any promise-breakers

C. He forced them to give a public donation to the poor

D. He asked the prophets to pronounce a curse on them

9. What was Nehemiah's approach to his role as governor in terms of generosity?

A. He demanded a food allowance from the people

B. He regularly made lavish public displays of wealth

C. He declined a food allowance and provided for 150 people daily at his own expense

D. He only provided food to foreign dignitaries

10. What did Nehemiah ask God to do at the end of chapter 5?

A. To bless the wealth of the nobles

B. To remember his actions for the good of the people

C. To punish the poor for their complaints

D. To bring more hardship to the people for their sins

What Do You Say?

How do Nehemiah's actions on behalf of the poor challenge our approach to justice, wealth, and leadership in our own communities?

LESSON 10

Conspiracy, but the Work Gets Finished

Nehemiah 6—7

Introduction

In previous lessons in the book of Nehemiah we learned that Sanballat was a fierce and sinister enemy of Israel. He hated to see the wall of Jerusalem being rebuilt. At first, he tried to stop the project by ridiculing the workers. When that tactic didn't work, he assembled the army of Samaria to fight against the workers. However, that tactic didn't work either. In this lesson, we will see Sanballat employ another tactic. He was as persistent as he was evil. However, Nehemiah was persistent too. Every time Sanballat tried to stop the rebuilding of the wall, Nehemiah prayed and kept on building.

Nehemiah responds to the first conspiracy (6:1–4)

Nehemiah and his builders had many enemies: Sanballat, Tobiah, Geshem the Arab, and others. These enemies heard that the wall had progressed to the point that there were no gaps, although the doors and gates still needed to be hung (6:1). Sanballat and Geshem suggested that Nehemiah meet them at Hakkephirim, a village, on the plain of Ono, about 25 miles northwest of Jerusalem. Nehemiah, in his wisdom, knew his enemies intended to harm him (6:2), so he sent messengers to them with a flat refusal. He told them he was doing a great work and saw no reason to leave it to meet with them (6:3).

Often, the enemies of the gospel try to distract believers from doing the Lord's work. We should refuse to be distracted and continue doing what the Lord wants us to do. Jesus cautioned that "No one who puts his hand to the plow and looks back is fit for the kingdom of God" (Luke 9:62).

Nehemiah's enemies were persistent. They extended their invitation to meet with them four more times, but Nehemiah answered each invitation the same way. He told them he was doing a great work and could not meet with them (6:4). We cannot expect the Devil, our enemy, to stop trying to lure us away from serving the Lord. He will tempt us until we take our last breath and enter heaven. We need to follow Nehemiah's example and keep on doing the Lord's work. Jesus told the church at Smyrna: "Be faithful unto death, and I will give you the crown of life" (Revelation 2:10).

Nehemiah responds to the second conspiracy (6:5–9)

Sanballat schemed another way to stop the building of the wall. This was his fifth attempt to halt the wall's construction. He wrote a counterfeit letter and gave it to his servant to carry to Nehemiah (6:5). The letter charged that it was reported among the nations and agreed to by Geshem that Nehemiah and his fellow Jews were building the wall in order to rebel. Furthermore, the letter charged that Nehemiah wanted to be the Jews' king (6:6). Of course, Nehemiah had no such ambition, but they knew that the King of Persia would take the threat to his authority seriously. A few centuries later Jesus' enemies ridiculed Him when He hung on the cross. The Pharisees hated Jesus for the authority He commanded, though He did not claim His rightful title as their king. This threat led to their conspiracy to have Jesus crucified. As He died, they made fun of His identity as King of the Jews (Luke 23:36-38). Nevertheless, Jesus was rightfully the King of Israel (see John 1:49, 12:12–15).

Sanballat's open letter also said Nehemiah had appointed prophets to proclaim that he was Israel's king (Nehemiah 6:7). The letter sounded a serious threat to Nehemiah by saying the reports about Nehemiah would reach the King of Persia (6:7). In view of all the charges in the letter, Sanballat suggested that Nehemiah meet him so they could discuss the matter (6:7). Undoubtedly, Sanballat wanted Nehemiah to think that he would come up with a plan to rescue Nehemiah from a perilous situation. However, if Nehemiah accepted the offer to confer with Sanballat, he would not return to Jerusalem alive.

Wisely, Nehemiah rejected Sanballat's offer and denied all the accusations against him. He accused Sanballat of making these things up in his own mind (6:8). He saw that the letter was a sinister scheme to frighten him and the builders of the wall so that they would abandon the project. Instead of having the talk with Sanballat, Nehemiah talked to God. He prayed, "But now, O God, strengthen my hands" (6:9).

Prayer is always the best way to respond to adversity. Philippians 4:6, 7 presents prayer as the way to escape anxiety and enjoy peace.

Nehemiah responds to the third conspiracy (6:10–14)

Nehemiah visited Shemaiah in his home, perhaps to console him because Shemaiah was house bound. But Shemaiah suggested the two men meet in the temple behind closed doors. He claimed that doing so would protect Nehemiah from his enemies (6:10). Nehemiah rejected this suggestion. He knew the Lord would not ask him to do what only priests were allowed to do (6:11; see Numbers 3:10; 18:7). He also discerned that Tobiah and Sanballat had hired Shemaiah to draw him into a trap (6:12). Their evil scheme was supposed to make Nehemiah afraid and become the object of the Jews' disdain (6:13). Once again, Nehemiah prayed. He prayed for God's judgment on Tobiah, Sanballat, the prophetess Noadiah and the other prophets who had schemed to make him afraid (6:14). Although Christians are not told to desire judgment on their enemies (Proverbs 24:17-18), they are exhorted to pray (Philippians 4:6) and God will answer according to His perfect, holy and good will.

Being betrayed by a friend is almost unthinkable, but you may recall that Judas, a so-called friend, betrayed Jesus. He led a group of arresting soldiers into the garden, where Jesus was praying, and identified Jesus to them by greeting Jesus with a kiss (Matthew 26:47-49). Here again we see Nehemiah's experience in parallel with Jesus'.

The wall completed (6:15-19)

Nehemiah 6:15–19 reports good news and bad news. The good news is the wall was finished in 52 days and Nehemiah's enemies were afraid and realized that the builders had succeeded with God's help (6:15, 16). The bad news is some of Judah's officials carried on correspondence with Tobiah (6:17). These officials had vowed allegiance to Tobiah because he was related to them (6:18). They bragged about Tobiah to Nehemiah and told Tobiah what Nehemiah said. Tobiah responded to Nehemiah with threatening letters (6:19).

The Bible makes it clear that we should not enter into any partnership with the enemies of the cross in any religious endeavor (Philippians 3:18; 2 Corinthians 6:14–18). False teachers may try to befriend us, but their goal, like the goal of Nehemiah's enemies, is to harm us and destroy our faith, or use us for their own gain. Religious teachers are false if they deny these fundamentals of the faith:

- The Bible is the verbally (word for word) inspired Word of God. (2 Peter 1:20-21)
- Jesus is the virgin born, sinless Son of God, perfect man and perfect God. (1 John 4:1-3)
- Jesus performed real miracles. (John 14:11)
- Jesus shed His blood for our sins. (Ephesians 1:7)
- Jesus arose bodily from the dead. (1 Corinthians 15:14-15)
- Jesus is coming again. (1 Thessalonians 5)

The following poem emphasizes the differences between right beliefs and false beliefs.

"You're just out of date,"
said young pastor Bate
To one of our faithful old preachers
Who had tarried for years in travail and tears
The gospel to poor sinful creatures.
"You still preach on Hades,
and shock cultured ladies
With your barbarous doctrine of blood!
You're so far behind you will never catch up—
You're a flat tire stuck in the mud!"
For some little while, a bit of a smile
Enlightened the old preacher's face.
Being made the butt of ridicule's cut
Did not ruffle his sweetness and grace.
Then he returned to young Bate,
so suave and sedate.
"Catch up, did my ears hear you say'
"Why, I couldn't succeed if I doubled my speed,

"My friend, I'm not going your way!"

—Anonymous

Nehemiah makes post-construction arrangements (7:1–73)

After the wall was built, the doors had been hung in the gates, and the gatekeepers, temple singers, and Levites had been appointed (7:1), Nehemiah put his brother Hanani and Hananiah, a reliable and God-fearing man, in charge of Jerusalem (7:2). You may recall that Hanani had told Nehemiah about Jerusalem's ruins when Nehemiah was the Persian king's cupbearer. Nehemiah charged the two men with the security of the gates (7:3). Only a few people were living in the big city of Jerusalem, and none of the houses that were destroyed by the Babylonians had been rebuilt (7:4). Believing that God wanted him to assemble the nobles and the officials and the people to be enrolled, Nehemiah began with a list of those who had returned with Zerubbabel (7:5–7). The people were listed according to their families and clans, and Nehemiah even counted the animals (7:8–69).

The chapter ends by noting that the people, including Nehemiah himself, donated large sums of gold and silver to the treasury as well as 67 priests' garments (7:70–72). Following the assembly, the people settled in their ancestral towns (7:73). Again, this list of names shows that God does not lose track of any of us, and does not leave any person out of His accounts. Although Nehemiah's enrollment was important, enrollment in the Book of Life (Revelation 20:15) is far more important. Those, whose names are written there, have eternal life through faith in Jesus Christ (John 3:36). Is your name written there?

LESSON 10 EXAM

Use the answer sheet that has been provided to complete your exam.

1. What was Sanballat's first attempt to stop Nehemiah and the rebuilding of the wall?

A. He spread false rumors about Nehemiah's intentions
B. He ridiculed the workers
C. He sent an army to attack Jerusalem
D. He bribed the workers to stop building

2. How did Nehemiah respond to the repeated invitations from Sanballat and Geshem to meet at Ono?

A. He agreed to meet with them in secret
B. He ignored their invitations completely
C. He refused, saying he was doing a great work and could not leave
D. He accepted the invitation to discuss the matter

3. What was the main accusation in the counterfeit letter sent by Sanballat to Nehemiah?

A. Nehemiah was building the wall to rebel against Persia
B. Nehemiah was planning to attack neighboring cities
C. Nehemiah had stolen from the poor
D. Nehemiah had abandoned his post as governor

4. What was Nehemiah's response when he received the false letter from Sanballat?

A. He accepted the invitation and went to meet Sanballat
B. He called for an assembly to address the issue
C. He retaliated with a public announcement
D. He prayed to God for strength and denied the accusations

5. What was Shemaiah's suggestion to Nehemiah in the third conspiracy?

A. Nehemiah should pray for the enemies
B. Nehemiah should meet with Sanballat in secret
C. Nehemiah should flee to the temple for protection
D. Nehemiah should attack the enemies head-on

6. Why did Nehemiah reject Shemaiah's suggestion to flee to the temple?

A. He knew it was unlawful for him, a non-priest, to enter the temple in that way

B. He was afraid of being captured

C. He did not want to disrupt the work on the wall

D. He feared the enemies would ambush him at the temple

7. How long did it take Nehemiah and the workers to complete the wall?

A. 30 days

B. 52 days

C. 6 months

D. 1 year

8. What did Nehemiah do after the wall was completed?

A. He celebrated a feast

B. He appointed his brother and Hananiah to guard the city

C. He invited all the neighboring nations to join him

D. He returned to Persia

9. What issue did Nehemiah discover about the officials of Judah after the wall was finished?

A. They were stealing from the treasury

B. They were plotting against the king of Persia

C. They were communicating with Tobiah, one of the enemies

D. They were neglecting their duties

10. What does the census in Nehemiah 7 remind us of in terms of God's care for His people?

A. God forgets no one and keeps a record of all who belong to Him

B. God's work is only for a few chosen people

C. God's people are always in danger of being lost

D. God is only concerned with the wealthy and powerful

What Do You Say?

How can we stay focused when distractions or false accusations come our way?

LESSON 11

The Power of God's Word

Nehemiah 8—10

Introduction

In this lesson our focus falls on Ezra the scribe. God had used Nehemiah as a builder to rally the people around the task of rebuilding Jerusalem's wall. Next, God used Ezra to rally the people around the task of rebuilding their lives and their devotion to the law of Moses. Not surprisingly, Ezra who initiated this revival "had set his heart to study the Law of the Lord, and to do it and to teach his statutes and rules in Israel" (Ezra 7:10).

Ezra reads the Law of Moses to the people (8:1–8)

For some reason the people gathered near the Water Gate and asked Ezra, the scribe and priest, to bring the Book of the Law of Moses, the first five books the Bible (8:1). Perhaps this interest in the Law of Moses occurred because the people had seen how the Lord had protected them and enabled them to complete the building of the wall. Whatever the reason, it was commendable that they wanted to hear God's Word. So, on the first day of the seventh month, which was the time of the Feast of Trumpets (Leviticus 23:24; Numbers 29:1), from early morning to midday, Ezra read from the Law of Moses to all who could understand. During all that time, the people listened attentively (Nehemiah 8:2, 3).

Ezra and thirteen others stood on a platform that had been built for the occasion (8:4). During the reading, the people stood (8:4, 5). Can you picture people today standing for about five hours to hear someone read God's Word? Obviously, the people who heard Ezra read the Law must have been hungry for it!

Following the reading, Ezra praised God, and the people responded by exclaiming, "Amen, Amen." They lifted up their hands, bowed their heads, and worshiped the Lord (8:6). To help the audience understand what Ezra read, certain Levites read from the Book of the Law and explained what it meant (8:8). This is still a model we need! Pastors today should follow the Levites' example by helping people understand clearly what God's Word says. The apostle Paul urged Timothy to "preach the word" (2 Timothy 4:2). He also told Titus that an elder "must hold firm to the trustworthy word as taught, so that he may be able to give instruction in sound doctrine and also to rebuke those who contradict it" (Titus 1:9).

The people observe the Feast of Booths (8:9–18)

While the Law of Moses was being read, all the people wept. Likely, hearing the Law caused them to see they had disobeyed its commandments. Nevertheless, Nehemiah, Ezra and the Levites told them not to weep because the day was holy to the Lord (8:9). Nehemiah instructed the crowd to go home, feast, give to the needy, and rejoice, because the joy of the Lord is their strength (8:10). There is a time for rejoicing and a time for mourning (Ecclesiastes 3:4), as we will see in the next chapter. The Levites quieted the crowd and told them not to grieve but to observe the day as holy (8:11). In response, the people returned home to do as they had been instructed (8:12).

The following day the leaders of the clans, the priests, and the Levites came to Ezra to study the Law (8:13). They learned that the Feast of Booths was to be celebrated from the 15th day to the 22nd day of the seventh month (8:13, 14), at which time the people would dwell in booths made from tree branches (Leviticus 23:37–43; Nehemiah 8:14). So, the returnees from the captivity gathered branches, made booths, and lived in booths for the allotted time (8:1, 16). This was the first time since the time of Joshua that the entire assembly of Israel celebrated the Feast of Booths, and they did so with great joy (8:17).

Every day during the Feast of Booths, Ezra read from the Book of the Law in accordance with the instruction in Deuteronomy 31:10–13 (Nehemiah 8:18). The following day, the people gathered in a solemn assembly (8:18).

A day of confession, and retelling Israel's history (9:1–37)

Two days after the Feast of Booths the people gathered together with great remorse (9:1). They separated themselves from all foreigners, stood, and confessed their sins and the sins of their ancestors (9:2). They spent the day reading the Book of the Law, confessing. and worshiping (9:3). As we read God's Word, we learn that we have sinned. We also learn to confess our sin and turn our hearts toward God in worship. A group of Levites stood on the stairs, perhaps the stairs that led up to the platform, and praised the Lord (9:4, 5). They described the Lord as Israel's everlasting God. They said His name is glorious and exalted above all blessing and praise. When we worship the Lord, we should acknowledge His glory and majesty. He is far more worthy of any praise we might ascribe to Him. He created the universe and sustains it (9:6). Colossians 1:17 teaches us that Jesus Christ, God's preeminent Son, holds the universe together.

The Levites' prayer and praise continued with a review of Israel's history, beginning with Abram. God called him out of the idolatrous city of Ur (Genesis 12:1), a well-developed city on the Euphrates River. The Lord changed Abram's name (which means "father is exalted") to Abraham ("father of a great multitude) and promised to give him the land of Canaan (15:7, 17–21). The Levites also spoke about the Lord's deliverance of His people from Egypt and that He parted the Red Sea for them but drowned the pursuing Egyptians (Nehemiah 9:9–11). Furthermore, the Levites recalled the Lord's miraculous guidance of His people in the wilderness (9:12) and His gift of the Law at Mount Sinai (9:13-14). He also gave them bread from heaven, water from a rock, and commanded them to enter the Promised Land and possess it (9:15).

In spite of all the Lord did for them, the Israelites disobeyed Him and forgot the miracles He performed on their behalf (9:16, 17).They even wanted to return to Egypt, but the Lord, who is ready to forgive, gracious, merciful, and infinitely loving, did not abandon them, not even when they made a golden calf to worship (9:18, 19). He kept on providing for them and guiding them so that they needed nothing (9:20, 21). He even made them victorious over their enemies (9:22). God is truly gracious!

The Levites recalled that the Lord brought His people into the

Promised Land and enabled them to defeat the Canaanites and take possession of their cities and fruitful land (9:23–25). Nevertheless, the people rebelled against the Lord. They killed His prophets and committed blasphemies (9:26).

We should recall the Lord's goodness to us and respond appropriately. "Oh, give thanks to the Lord, for He is good! For His mercy endures forever" (1 Chronicles 16:34).

The Levites' prayer continued to recall Israel's history of rebellion and cruelty at the hands of their enemies, but they also highlighted the Lord's mercy to the present time. However, they told the Lord that, after returning to their homeland, they were slaves in it. This was a reference to the taxes they paid to the King of Persia (see Nehemiah 9:27–37).

A written -promise made to the Lord (9:38—10:39)

The Levites' prayer ended on a high note; the Levites, princes and priests signed an agreement to obey the Law of Moses (9:38; 10:1–29). Those that signed the promise included the Jews' leaders, the priests, the Levites, the gatekeepers, the singers, the temple servants, and all the people (10:1–28). Again, their names are recorded. They invoked a curse if they failed to keep the Law of Moses, which they vowed to observe (10:29). They pledged that they would not allow their children to marry Gentiles (10:30). They also vowed they would not buy from the Gentiles on the Sabbath or on a holy day (10:31). Furthermore, they pledged to observe the sabbatical year (10:31). In addition, they said they would give to the Lord what the Law of Moses demanded; nor would they neglect the temple (10:32–39).

These oaths were solemn oaths that the people would not be able to keep in their own strength. They needed God's grace to fulfill their promises. Jesus came to fulfill the Law, knowing that He alone could free those who were under the law (Galatians 3:13; 5:1). No doubt we all make promises to the Lord, but we must rely on His grace and the power of the Holy Spirit to fulfill them. The Lord has set us free from striving to please Him in our own strength so that we can please Him by living by faith (Hebrews 11:6). Christians, too, sometimes make promises to the Lord. It is important to keep these promises. Ecclesiastes 5:4 reads: "When you vow a vow to God, do not delay paying it, for he has no pleasure in fools."

LESSON 11 EXAM

Use the answer sheet that has been provided to complete your exam.

1. Who played a central role in encouraging the people to return to the Law of Moses?

A. Nehemiah
B. Ezra
C. The Levites
D. The priests

2. Where did the people gather to hear the reading of the Law of Moses?

A. The Temple
B. The Water Gate
C. The King's Palace
D. The marketplace

3. How long did Ezra read the Law of Moses to the people on the first day?

A. One hour
B. Two hours
C. From morning to midday
D. All day long

4. What did the people do in response to hearing the reading of the Law?

A. They immediately began to argue
B. They wept and mourned
C. They stood in silence
D. They celebrated with a feast

5. What did Nehemiah and Ezra tell the people to do after they wept?

A. To repent and fast
B. To rejoice and celebrate
C. To leave the city and go home
D. To make sacrifices in the temple

6. What festival did the people begin to observe after hearing the Law?

A. The Feast of Booths
B. The Passover
C. The Feast of Tabernacles
D. The Day of Atonement

7. How did the Levites help the people understand the Law?

A. They gave public speeches
B. They offered sacrifices
C. They explained the Law to the people
D. They led the people in worship

8. What did the people do after confessing their sins?

A. They made a burnt offering
B. They wrote a letter of repentance
C. They sang songs of worship
D. They signed an agreement to follow the Law

9. Which of the following did the people vow to do in their written agreement?

A. To rebuild the temple
B. To allow their children to marry Gentiles
C. To observe the sabbatical year
D. To stop giving tithes and offerings

10. What is a key lesson from the Levites' prayer and the people's confession in Nehemiah 9?

A. The importance of sacrifices in the temple
B. The grace and mercy of God in forgiving His people
C. The necessity of building a new temple
D. The power of following the king's commands

What Do You Say?

What does it mean to truly repent, and how is it different from just feeling sorry for our actions?

LESSON 12

Settling Down and Taking Responsibility

Nehemiah 11—13

Introduction

Nehemiah did not shy away from his responsibilities. He served in Persia as the king's faithful cupbearer. As the cupbearer, he was responsible for the king's safety. He tasted what the king was going to drink. If the drink contained poison. Nehemiah would die, but the king would live. Nehemiah faithfully assumed that life or death responsibility.

When he believed God wanted him to return to Jerusalem to rebuild its ruined wall, he did not shrink from the responsibility to do so. He bravely asked the king for permission to leave.

In Jerusalem, he took on the responsibility of organizing the builders of the wall and to supervise its construction. Even threats on his life did not deter him from carrying out his mission.

In this lesson, once again we see Nehemiah taking responsibility to appoint choirs and to bring about much-needed reforms in Judah.

Before we study Nehemiah's reforms, let's observe that the Jews settled into their homes.

Settling down to live in Jerusalem and the surrounding area (11:1–36)

The leaders of the people lived in Jerusalem, and the people cast lots for one tenth of the population to live in Jerusalem, "the holy city" (11:1). The other people settled in neighboring villages (11:1–36).

It must have been exciting for the people of Jerusalem and Judah to move into their homes. Homes provide a sense of belonging and a feeling of comfort and security. Christians do not have a permanent home in this life, but look forward to their permanent home in the next. Jesus said we are not of the world (John 17:14). The apostle Peter wrote that we are "sojourners and exiles" (1 Peter 2:11); and Paul wrote that "our citizenship is in heaven" (Philippians 3:20). Someday we will settle into rooms that Jesus, the carpenter of Nazareth, is preparing for us in the Father's house (John 14:1–3). He promised to come again and take us to that wonderful place. Just as the excitement of the Jews return to their homes in Jerusalem propelled them to seek and obey the Lord, the expectation of His return for us (and our new homes with Him) should prompt us to live in a moment-by-moment dedication to Him (see 1 John 3:2, 3).

A list of priests and Levites (12:1–26)

Nehemiah began his list of priests and Levites with those who accompanied Zerubbabel when he returned to Jerusalem from Babylon. Jeshua, the high priest, is named first (12:1). These priests arrived in Jerusalem about one hundred years before Nehemiah. Twenty-two are listed (12:1).

Next, Nehemiah listed the Levites who returned with Zerubbabel (12:8, 9). He included the temple singers, including those who were in charge of the songs of thanksgiving.

In Nehemiah 12:10, 11 we find the names of high priests. Joiakim was the father of Jeshua, the high priest who returned with Zerubbabel (12:10; Ezra 2:1, 2). Eliashib served as high priest in Nehemiah's time (13:4, 7, 28). Nehemiah 12:12–21 lists the heads of priestly families in the time of Jeshua's son Joiakim.

The heads of Levite families as well as the priests in the time of King Darius of Persia were listed in the official Levite records (12:23). The Levites who served in the time of Joiakim, the high priest, and in the time of Ezra and Nehemiah are named in Nehemiah 12:24–26). The gatekeepers' names are also listed in verse 25. Once again, Scripture shows us the diligent record keeping of God and His attention to individuals. What lists will your name appear on?

The wall is dedicated (12:27–43)

The dedication of the wall was to be a joyful, grateful occasion. The Levites were called from their various towns to attend the dedication and to provide thanksgiving, singing, and music (12:27). The singers gathered from all around the region (12:28,29). This occasion was to be holy, therefore the priests and the Levites purified themselves, the people, the gates, and the wall (12:30). Likely, the priests sprinkled the blood of sacrificial animals on themselves, on the people, on the gates, and on the wall.

God is the giver of everything we possess. Even our bodies are not our own; they belong to Him. He purchased them, and therefore we should use our bodies to glorify Him (1 Corinthians 6:19, 20). Paul exhorts us to dedicate our bodies and minds to God (Romans 12:1, 2). And just as joy accompanied the dedication of Jerusalem's wall, so we should joyfully dedicate ourselves and all that we have to Him.

Nehemiah brought Judah's leaders onto the wall and appointed two great choirs to give thanks. A procession led by Ezra traveled south to the Dung Gate and proceeded to the Water Gate (12:31, 37). The procession included half of Judah's leaders, priests with trumpets. Zechariah and eight of his relatives followed with musical instruments (12:32–36).

The second choir that gave thanks to the Lord walked north and then east. Finally, the two choirs met in the temple (12:40). The choirs, Nehemiah, half the officials, and half the people on the wall followed the choir to the Gate of the Guard (12:38–39). Both choirs stood in the temple along with Nehemiah and half of the officials (12:40). Seven priests offered great sacrifices and everyone, including the women and children, rejoiced so loudly that the sound of joy was heard far away (12:41–43).

Interestingly, the act of so many people walking on the wall refuted Tobiah's claim that the walls would crumble under the weight of a fox (Nehemiah 4:3). Tobiah and Sanballat may have watched in silence as the processions on the wall took place. Taunts and insults cannot thwart any work that God oversees.

Preparations for temple worship (12:44–47)

Nehemiah arranged for side rooms in the temple to be available for the people's tithes and contribution (12:44, 45). He also made certain that the priests and Levites ministered according to the order David established more than five centuries earlier (see 1 Chronicles 22-26). The priests, Levites, singers, and gatekeepers ministered according to the command of David and Solomon (Nehemiah 12:45, 46), Nehemiah also showed his concern for right worship by having Israel maintain daily provisions for the singers, the gatekeepers, and the Levites (12:47).

Nehemiah enacts reforms (13:1–31)

The Word of God had a profound effect on the people of Israel. When they heard from the Law of Moses that Ammonites and Moabites were barred from the temple (see Deuteronomy 23:3–6), they excluded the foreigners from Israel (Nehemiah 13:1–3). The Ammonites and Moabites had opposed Israel's journey to Canaan and had hired Balaam to curse Israel (see Numbers 22:1–6).

When Nehemiah was back in Persia (Nehemiah 13:6), Eliashib, the high priest, had prepared a room in the temple for Tobiah, the Ammonite (13:4, 5). Upon his return to Jerusalem, Nehemiah learned what Eliashib had done (13:7). He became enraged and threw all of Tobiah's furniture out of the temple and gave orders to cleanse the temple (13:8). Then he restored the holy vessels, the grain offering, and the frankincense to the temple (13:9).

Nehemiah also discovered that the people had not provided for the Levites and the singers. Therefore, the Levites and singers had left the temple and gone home (13:10). Perhaps this lack of provision for the Levites and singers had left the storerooms empty so that Eliashib was able to build a room there for Tobiah.

We can only imagine what would happen to a church if its people stopped giving. Although believers are not commanded specifically to tithe (give 10 percent of their income) to the Lord's work, shouldn't we give at least that amount? We are exhorted to give cheerfully as the Lord has prospered us (1 Corinthians 16:2; 2 Corinthians 9:7).

After learning that the people had not supported the Levites and the singers, Nehemiah corrected the situation. He confronted the officials, reinstated the Levites and the singers, and chose reliable men to oversee the tithing (Nehemiah 13:11–13). Also, he prayed that what he had done would not come to nothing (13:14).

Next, Nehemiah put an end to merchants selling their goods on the Sabbath. He warned that he would lay hands on them if he caught them doing it. Furthermore, he ordered the Levites to purify themselves and guard the gates. Again, he prayed (13:15–22).

Finally, Nehemiah confronted Jews who had married Gentile women. He cursed some of them, pulled out their hair, and made them vow not to let their children marry the Gentiles (13:23–25). He reminded them that Solomon's foreign wives caused him to sin (13:26).

Nehemiah chased the high priest's grandson away, because he was Sanballat's son-in-law (13:28). He turned over to divine judgment those who had desecrated the priesthood and the covenant they had made earlier to obey the Law of Moses (13:29). Then he assigned duties to the priests and Levites (13:30). He also made sure that wood and first fruits arrived at the temple. He prayed once again that his God would remember him— not let his work come to nothing (13:31)

Nehemiah's zeal for protecting the temple pictures our Lord's zeal for the temple in His day. He cleansed the temple by driving out the merchants, whose corrupt money-making business had polluted the temple. He emphasized that the Lord's house was to be a house of prayer (Luke 19:45, 46; John 2:13–17). Although our zeal for our places of worship cannot match our Lord's, it should be demonstrated in faithful attendance (Hebrews 10:25) and worship in spirit and truth (John 4:24).

The book of Nehemiah demonstrates God's grace and power in setting His people free from bondage in Babylon to rebuild Jerusalem's temple and wall. But He also demonstrated His grace and power to rebuild His people's lives through the dedicated ministries of Ezra and Nehemiah. Surely, He can do something similar today by rebuilding civilizations, individual lives, and homes. He has set us Christians free to play a part in His rebuilding program.

LESSON 12 EXAM

Use the answer sheet that has been provided to complete your exam.

1. Why did Nehemiah organize the people to settle in Jerusalem?
A. To fulfill a prophecy
B. To increase Jerusalem's population
C. To ensure the protection and rebuilding of the city
D. To accommodate all of the Jews returning from exile

2. What did Nehemiah do to celebrate the dedication of the wall?
A. He held a large feast
B. He organized two choirs to give thanks and celebrated with sacrifices
C. He built a monument
D. He offered a series of prayers

3. Who were the Levites who played a key role in the dedication of the wall?
A. The gatekeepers and singers
B. Ezra and Nehemiah
C. The priests who offered sacrifices
D. The leaders of the twelve tribes

4. What did Nehemiah discover about the temple after he returned from Persia?
A. The temple was being misused by outsiders
B. The Levites had abandoned their duties
C. The temple was completely destroyed
D. The people were no longer worshipping

5. Why was Nehemiah angered when he returned to Jerusalem?
A. The temple had been destroyed
B. People were desecrating the Sabbath
C. Tobiah the Ammonite had been given a room in the temple
D. The people had stopped giving offerings

6. What reform did Nehemiah implement regarding the Sabbath?

A. He allowed merchants to sell on the Sabbath if they were Jewish.

B. He instituted fasting on the Sabbath

C. He expanded the Sabbath to include other days.

D. He closed the gates on the Sabbath to prevent merchants from selling.

7. How did Nehemiah respond to those who had married foreign women?

A. He ignored the issue

B. He celebrated their marriages

C. He rebuked and cursed some of them, pulling out their hair

D. He encouraged mixed marriages for peace

8. What role did the people play in the dedication of the wall?

A. They attended and celebrated but did not participate actively

B. They were involved in a prayer vigil

C. They participated in the joyful procession, sacrifices, and worship

D. They helped in rebuilding the wall

9. How did Nehemiah ensure that the temple's worship was sustained after his reforms?

A. He sent the people to foreign lands to gather resources

B. He reinstated the Levites and singers to their roles and secured provisions

C. He focused on building additional temples

D. He removed all the priests from the temple

10. What was Nehemiah's final prayer at the end of the book?

A. That God would forgive his sins

B. That God would remember his deeds and not let his work come to nothing

C. That the people would be restored to their land

D. That God would bless Jerusalem forever

What Do You Say?

How can we, as individuals and a community, incorporate more joyful celebration and worship into our everyday lives, especially when we experience God's faithfulness in the midst of challenges?